New Faces
of Leadership

New Faces
of Leadership

Amanda Sinclair
and
Valerie Wilson

MELBOURNE UNIVERSITY PRESS

MELBOURNE UNIVERSITY PRESS
PO Box 278, Carlton South, Victoria 3053, Australia
mup-info@unimelb.edu.au
www.mup.com.au

First published 2002
Text © Amanda Sinclair and Valerie Wilson 2002
Design and typography © Melbourne University Press 2002

Typeset in 10 point Giovanni Book by Syarikat Seng Teik Sdn. Bhd., Malaysia
Printed in Australia by McPherson's Printing Group

National Library of Australia Cataloguing-in-Publication entry

Sinclair, Amanda, 1953– .
  New faces of leadership.
  Bibliography.
  Includes index.
  ISBN 0 522 85035 9.

  1. Leadership. 2. Success in business. 3. Executive ability. I. Wilson, Valerie, 1947– . II. Title
658.4092

Contents

Acknowledgements

Our first thanks go to our interviewees, who were reflective and expansive about experiences of difference in their lives and careers. Just to be different, in reverse alphabetical order they are Wilson Wu, Bruce Thompson, Seng Tan, Carol Schwartz, George Savvides, Neville Roach, Pauline Pereira, Helmut Pekarek, Sir Arvi Parbo, Colin O'Reilly, Roland Orchard, Mike Oppenheimer, Shane O'Hart, Norry McAllister, Alistair Maitland, Jonathan Ling, Thomas Lau, Bob Johnston, Tracey Horton, Chris Furtado, Peter Duncan, Nuno D'Aquino, Ric Clark, Frank Cicutto, Chris Childs, Walter Bugno, Tom Brown, Greg Bourne, Rita Avdiev and Veronica Allen. We also thank those who suggested contacts for our work, particularly Clarence da Gama Pinto, Hass Dellal, Jenny McGregor and Neville Roach. The Department of Immigration and Multicultural Affairs provided the catalyst and financial support for the research component of this book. In particular, Dr Thuy Nguyen-Hoan, Phil Rabl and Randal White were encouraging and supportive of our work. Members of the Inter Company Network and the Corporate Diversity Think Tank have facilitated our access to interviewees and provided valuable feedback on interim findings. We would also like to thank and acknowledge the assistance of the whole Productive Diversity Partnership group, whose ideas and feedback have enriched our insights.

Our research focused on diversity. If there is a single conclusion we took from our work it is the need to locate an appreciation of difference and diversity in a much wider, and deeper, context. Making connections from what we were hearing to backgrounds and histories, and often to taboo subjects in business such as race and prejudice, have been the pleasure and challenge of this work.

We would like to thank our families and friends for their interest and support throughout our excavations.

Amanda Sinclair and Valerie Britton Wilson

Changing faces of leadership: new tasks, new contexts, new faces

This is a book about corporate leadership of a different kind. The leaders described here don't fit the traditional template, where leaders are tough, out-front, self-reliant, masculine. That mould has come to circumscribe our understandings of corporate leadership. The leaders we describe in this book are very successful men and women. Some are high-profile leaders of major corporations. Some are not well-known. Yet we believe that it is to this sort of person we must look to map the changing face of leadership.

The heroic model of leadership that has so dominated management thinking is dangerously out of touch with the dynamic and diverse reality of organisational life. The model limits our understanding of what constitutes successful leadership, it actively suppresses experimentation and innovation in leadership practice and it acts as a disincentive to people who don't fit the mould of self-reliant individualism.

The leaders we introduce in this book have important things to tell us about the changing challenges of leadership. Our focus is on leaders who are experienced in managing across borders and boundaries. Some of those borders have been physical, national borders. Others have crossed borders that are less tangible but equally powerful—linguistic, socio-economic, familial and emotional borders. We demonstrate the continuing relevance of their varied experiences in forging the ingredients for successful leadership. The attribute we have termed 'border-crossing' is increasingly important in the twenty-first century business environment where 'global literacies' (Rosen 2000) and emotional literacies (Goleman 1998; Little 1999) matter more than traditional technical skills or knowledge.

The new practices of leadership that emerge from our exploration of the pathways and styles of these leaders are more anti-heroic than heroic. These leaders are attuned to others and especially to working innovatively with, and learning from, others who are different. Less out-front than emergent, this leadership has the capacity and courage to follow a path that challenges the status quo.

As well as being a book about a different kind of leadership, this is a different kind of leadership book. The experiences and words of people who have come to leadership via unconventional paths occupy a central part of the book. We weave our analysis through leaders' own accounts of their experiences. We include their personal histories, demonstrating that in order to understand the development of leadership one needs to reconnect the person—their childhood and their history—to contemporary leadership practice.

Throughout the book we also argue that leadership can only be understood in its political, cultural and historical context. Our focus, on the one hand, looks inward—into the person—and on the other hand, looks outward—to the broader systemic context in which leadership is lauded or found wanting. Neither of these two perspectives sounds particularly radical. But in the field of leadership study, where texts and new 'truths' proliferate with alarming fecundity, re-attaching backgrounds and including structural contexts in analysis are rare starting points.

We begin with two leadership stories. These stories introduce the main themes of this book: how leaders develop their appetites and capabilities for working across traditional cultural and geographic borders; how they develop the vision to see contributions from new places and the courage to see beyond ethnocentrism and to work for greater openness to diversity in their organisations.

The backgrounds and personal histories of these less heroic corporate leaders reveal complex cultural *roots*. Leaders take multiple and varied *routes* towards an understanding of the new leadership task in a diverse, multicultural and global world. Leaders who come from disadvantaged or minority backgrounds, paradoxically, are reticent about their roots, their different cultural backgrounds and their border-crossing experiences. Their reticence is often with good reason, and we explore in a later chapter the pressures on leaders to censor their own experiences with 'being different'. While they may be impatient with the policy dogma of multiculturalism and diversity, these leaders bring their own experiences of being outsiders into they way they run their teams and organisations.

Louis Eduardo (pseudonym) comes from a very cosmopolitan background. Portuguese-Chinese, he grew up in Shanghai, his family having been Chinese traders for three generations. A great-great-grandfather had been Viceroy of Goa, and another branch of the family was established in Nagasaki. Six languages were spoken at home: two Chinese dialects, English, French, Portuguese, Russian and some Japanese as well. Louis was sent to the English school and his brother to the French school in Shanghai by a father committed to internationalism. He says this experience was formative:

> [it] formed my approach to life. I never had a problem dealing with any kind of grouping. [My biography] goes to the essence of what I do.

Expelled from Shanghai by the Communist regime, the family moved to Hong Kong and then to Australia, sponsored by some Australian business associates. They found themselves in rural New South Wales, the first and only Asian family that many of the local population had ever seen. Ironically, and paternalistically, it was they who were regarded as the 'primitives':

> they were amazed I knew how to use a knife and fork! We came from a centrally heated apartment in Hong Kong to a place where they were using chip heaters and wood ovens. Very primitive. One time the nuns called me out to show off my beautifully pleated shorts with silk lining. At that age I didn't want to be seen as different. [But] I have very happy memories, the neighbours always included us, except there was no work for Dad, so . . .

As a young man, resilience and determination to succeed were directed towards gaining acceptance. In the Australian culture of the 1950s, the route to manhood and belonging was through sport and sporting clubs. Louis grasped this head-on with typical optimism. The significance of his actions requires us to picture the context. We need to picture not just Australia but Queensland in the 1950s, where a particularly Anglo-Celtic homogeneity prevailed. Louis decides to join a surf club. The popular image of surf clubs then, as now, epitomised the Aussie macho thing: fit, tall, bronzed males, mostly blond and blue-eyed. But our new club member is short and stocky. He has brown eyes and he looks different, he looks Asian:

> In the last year of school, I joined a Surf Life Saving Club—the cultural turning point of my life. I figured if I wanted to be an Australian, I should make sure I'm assimilated as an Australian, and what more Australian thing can there be than surfing, and I love surfing and swimming anyway. So I hitchhiked down to the coast one day and just walked into a Surf Club and joined. The cultural strata of a surf club, everybody from a no-hoper to super-rich and you're taken to a common denominator, all sleep in dorms when you're away—you bond very strongly and I've stayed in that bonding ever since. I've still got very close ties with people in the surf club. The club became Number 1, I became an instructor, examiner, ran the District, on the Board, then State ... Once you were on one club you were adopted by all the others. In Sydney, I'd walk into Bondi and it would be open house.

This powerful bonding experience, he insists, ensured a degree of acceptance. However, the 'open house' of surfie culture did not extend to the corporate environments of the 1970s:

> I was sent to Melbourne and was talking to my manager to get time off to enrol in a Commerce degree. He said, 'Why do you want to do that?' I said, 'I want to get the degree and one day be General Manager'. He said, 'You'll never be GM. Number 1 you haven't gone to the right schools and number 2 you're not Anglo-Saxon'.
>
> I had a conversation with [his boss]. He was going to put me in a very senior position. I said he was totally wrong with what he was trying to do with the structure, and he said to me, 'Do you want to be in the A team or the B team?' I said I thought we were all one team. That was the last I heard of it, that particular job.

When they do well, leaders from an Asian background are often typecast as technical specialists and offered technical positions rather than those that might lead to general management or CEO. The following extract demonstrates vividly how 'thinking and being like us' can be used as a surrogate for 'general management material':

> Melbourne was difficult, there were strong old school networks and it was very cliquey. It was very hard to get to know people. I built my career through the technical side and it is more quantifiable than general management . . . I was indispensable from a technical point of view but was always sidetracked from general manager position. I chopped and changed jobs a lot without getting ahead because of the old school and racist thing.

This leader has recently retired as deputy CEO of one of Australia's best known companies, producing beer—that most revered and macho of Aussie products. He says he kept a low profile in the marketing of products and tended not to put himself forward as the public face of the company:

> General punters don't associate an Asian-looking face as head of such an Australian product. That's the only time I'm conscious of it. I appear in business publications but you rarely see my face in beer-type promotions. I'm a realist.

In contrast, Greg Williams grew up in outer urban Melbourne, the third son in a large family of boys. Providing a striking contrast to the cosmopolitan and colourful growing up of our first case, this leader's early years, at first glance, provide an infertile basis for an interest in moving beyond parochial borders. However, by adding in to our analysis some critical dimensions of growing up, such as relationships with parents, family structure and siblings, we see how the appetite for difference can be shaped through very different routes:

> I was always described as a 'bit different'. Mum was very conservative, I was more radical. So I was the kind of one likely to be doing something different compared with my brothers. I always did things that were a bit different, pushed the boundaries . . . My older brother was more like—we didn't really have a peer relationship—I saw him as part of the parental program [laughs]. He'd bring me into line from time to time . . . Dad was a bit of a tyrant, he used to deal out the punishment. He spent a lot of time with my oldest brother. They played cricket

together. They were out there doing their thing and I wasn't much involved in that. So, I probably had to find other ways to amuse myself [laughs].

This quote enables us to see how families and growing up can create the space to be different. The question of birth order— precisely where one is located in the family in relation to siblings —connects to issues about space, boundaries and relationships. Position in the family affects developing ideas about one's place in the world, about working with others and boundaries between self and other, inside and outside the family. Only children, first-borns, middle children, subsequent children, all will find different ways to connect with each other and with the world in general, its people and its objects.

In the case of this leader—and many others in our sample—the paternal influence that was strong for older children became diluted for those further down in the birth order. If this left a gap at the time, it also had some positive consequences, as the son felt less shackled by fatherly expectations, was able to be freer. There was also a sense that he was an 'observer' in the family, a bit detached, feeling slightly like an outsider.

After a happy and free almost-rural childhood, Greg Williams moved with his family to the suburbs and a pedestrian secondary school experience. His first job was as a storeman and packer in the firm his father had worked for and he recalls that he 'got wisdom pretty quickly when you start to realise what the options were ... Some of these guys are going to be doing this all their lives, but I'm not going to be one of them'.

It wasn't until he joined the firm where he later became Managing Director and was sent to work in Asia for several years that his appetite for difference was awakened. Equipped with a positive and optimistic outlook, he set about managing as he had done in Australia. He quickly confronted his own limitations. Organising a 'beer bust' or 'piss up' to celebrate the end of a good month, his Asian guests left as soon as the food stopped coming:

> I ordered all this grog from the American Club, just stacks of it ... and we had it catered, all this finger food. Everyone in the office turned up, ate all the food and then shot through. Didn't touch any grog at all, so here we were sitting in the cafeteria with enough for an army.

Greg had discovered to his embarrassment that his friendly attempts to replicate and transplant organisational rituals could misfire, looking crass and heavy-handed, and revealing the full inappropriateness of cultural assumptions.

In another example of cross-cultural learning, Greg made an assumption, when an employee came to tell him she was pregnant, that she was resigning:

> One of the assumptions I had that was ingrained in me because of my previous work experience was what women do in the workforce when they become pregnant. This is back in the 1980s I'm talking about now. One of the girls in the office came to let me know that she was pregnant. I said to her, 'Well, thanks very much for letting me know, good luck and would you help me choose your replacement'. Well she finished up in tears and I didn't know why and so I had to get someone to come and bail me out . . . I suddenly realised—how dumb is that— the norm in Taiwan is that you have the baby and you're home within three hours and back within a few weeks. The baby goes to the grand-parents and life goes on . . . I had absolutely no concept. I didn't even think about it.
>
> I found I had to make these really stupid errors to start understanding differences. I apologised to her later for my insensitivity. It was a learning experience that I still remember very vividly . . . at the time it was an embarrassment but then I started to think about all kinds of cultural differences that are not apparent. It was apparent that they're Chinese and I'm not, they're yellow and I'm white. That was obvious. But you don't know the extent of the difference by the obvious. You typically talk about food, religion, the day-to-day habits, but this got it to a different level. The incident enabled me to dig down . . . and we all became comfortable talking about differences that are not obvious . . .

The impact of making these errors and recognising his failures set Greg on a new path and with a new appetite for learning about difference and cultures. These experiences then positioned him differently in relation to his colleagues: for example, he developed an admiration for a Chinese boss which took him by surprise:

> I spent hours talking to him about the Chinese culture, the Chinese way of doing things, Chinese way of thinking, Confucian thinking . . . I think he appreciated that I tried to understand, I didn't just try to impose my management characteristics on his organisation . . . He's probably had as much effect on me as anyone in leadership. And I

didn't expect that. I thought I'd be the de facto leader—the white guy sent by the American head office—but nothing could be further from the truth.

It was a formative experience, changing him, his priorities and his style as a manager for the remainder of his career.

The new tasks of leadership

Despite the huge contrasts in these leaders' backgrounds and experiences, the summaries of their two stories introduce the key themes that are developed in this book: border-crossing, the experience of being an outsider, and what is made of it. What we discover are pointers to emerging forms of leadership that are different from the conventional heroic model.

The environment of business and of corporate leadership has changed dramatically and irrevocably in the past two or three decades. The need for growth, the universalisation of technologies and communications, the removal of some barriers to trade and the creation of markets that are ostensibly more open to competition have all fuelled an appetite for building business across borders. Some commentators have remarked that these new forms of ambition are not so different from traditional imperialism, beginning with the Romans and Chinese, who administered far-flung and often disparate imperial territories, and later the Hapsburg Empire and the British, in tandem with companies such as the East India Company.

What is different is the relative ease of moving goods and services around the world, of breaking up the chain of manufacture and delivery, making geography increasingly irrelevant. Doing business across national borders is part of the daily portfolio of a leader's tasks, whether in an Australian bank with a call centre in Delhi or a minerals company with the mining and processing of its materials separated by thousands of kilometres. Also, with the outsourcing of production to layers of contractors and sub-contractors in places far from head office, fewer and fewer large companies actually produce what they sell. Companies are investing more of their managerial energies into developing global brands than supervising shopfloors or coalfaces.

If we look at the evolution of managerial thinking through these periods of change, there was initially a rampant enthusiasm. This was an era when corporate chiefs simply calculated, and quoted, the size of, for example, the potential Chinese market, as justification for launching an operation there. 'We have to be there if we are to survive' was the imperative.

The management literature invited leaders and their companies to join a 'borderless' world in which corporate operation could be 'seamless'. Commentators predicted the death of national borders, and some management researchers confidently expected that cultural differences would dissolve in a shift towards a more standardised global economic culture (Levitt 1983). Single brands would sweep away cultural idiosyncrasies. 'It is critical to focus on the similarities, rather than the differences', preached one marketing guru, quite recently. 'Witness the global success of McDonald's, Coke, Proctor and Gamble' (Oliver 2000). In the Australian version of these scenarios, there has also been fear that domestic companies simply would not survive unless they extended their ambitions off-shore. Growth was the only strategy. And global growth at that.

But the experiences of Australian, European and American companies through the late 1980s and 1990s provided a dramatic reminder that cultural differences do matter. Whether it was in negotiating the red tape of Vietnamese or World Bank bureaucracy, or accommodating the preferences of Indonesian or Chinese markets, or seeking to run a production facility in Thailand or a bank in India, many companies found that management techniques and leadership approaches had to bend to at least respect, if not adjust to, cultural differences.

This finding also applies when companies establish operations in countries which seem, on the surface, to be similar. These days, most Australian-based and many American and European companies are much less sanguine about exporting a corporate culture, evolved and honed in the home country, to a variety of host cultures. Many Australian companies which have been successful in domestic and some limited overseas markets, are thinking very, very carefully before they commit to acquisitions or operations in places which lie well outside their cultural comfort zones.

At the same time, traditional approaches to international staffing through a cadre of expatriate managers are in decline. Transposed managers are exorbitant to maintain and often have high failure rates by a number of measures, and fewer and fewer high-quality managers want to live overseas and impose on their families the costs of expatriate lifestyle (Forster 2000). Multinational companies which have long relied on a group of permanent expatriate managers to run their businesses are looking at how to develop local talent in host country operations. But these transitions are delicate and by no means accomplished; they require levels of trust and capacities for devolution that are foreign to many corporate cultures. Some companies have responded by instituting extraordinarily tight levels of audit oversight and accountability.

These combinations of business conditions and leadership expectations, we argue, create radically new tasks for leaders. While there has been considerable debate about the economics and politics of globalisation, there has been insufficient work at the micro level, looking at how these issues play out for individual leaders and managers. An intensely competitive marketplace and pressures for growth, plus expectations that leaders will be able to lead across diverse cultures and increasingly diverse domestic workforces, together with the evidence that cultural differences continue to matter even as they evolve, are all good reasons to look more deeply at how leaders who come from a variety of backgrounds themselves are learning to lead in this changing business territory.

Studying leaders

In the study of leadership there have been two notable trends over the last few decades. The first trend has been a tendency by the business management literature to annex the leadership terrain. Where once the study of leadership was carried out in classics and politics departments, now one is much more likely to find professors of leadership in business and management schools. There has been a resulting tendency to conflate business leadership with other forms of leadership and to behave as if corporate leaders share the same characteristics with other sorts of leaders. This has produced theoretical and other problems in the study of leadership. Shamir (1995), in his study of charismatic leadership, points out that much of the research on charisma in corporate leaders has mistakenly extrapolated from studies of charismatic political and religious leaders. The key problem is that political and religious leaders benefit from being distant from followers and not having their charisma put to the close personal scrutiny that we typically measure when we are assessing corporate leaders. According to Shamir's study, close-up charismatic corporate leadership is a fundamentally different phenomenon from the more distant and managed charisma of political leaders.

At the same time that business leadership has come to be the main focus of leadership studies, another trend has been the study of leadership using the quantitative methodologies associated with psychology (Parry 1998). Rather than rely on history or biography, or detailed case studies which had been the political scientists' tools of trade, the field of leadership is now dominated by survey and questionnaire techniques and statistical analyses that trade off depth in favour of breadth. As Conger argues, 'most survey-generated leadership descriptors fail to help us understand the deeper structures of leadership phenomena. We trade-off the "how" and "why" questions about leadership for highly abstracted concepts and descriptions which allow us only to generalize . . . at relatively superficial levels' (109). Conger maintains that leadership, as a multiple-level and highly interpretive phenomenon, is much more suited to qualitative research methods, including interviews, observation and participant observation. A number of researchers who maintain the need for both qualitative and quantitative studies of leadership point out that despite thousands of quantitative studies, 'this general orientation has not yet led to an enduring and integrative theory of leadership' (Parry 1998; see also Yukl 1994 and Bennis and Nanus 1985).

The research presented here is concerned with the terrain of corporate leadership—the changing shape of the task of leading, and in particular the personal capabilities and strategies of being different and working with differences. In a corporate world characterised by the collapse of traditional boundaries and forecasts of borderless organisational operations, how do individual leaders negotiate? What capabilities do they mobilise to operate effectively in this environment?

These areas of interest—which are in their essence questions of identity and belonging—are increasingly well-traversed in contemporary literature (both fiction and non-fiction), in areas of cultural studies (particularly those which focus on post-colonial studies), and in a range of feminist and gay writing which is interested in how identity is constituted and transgressed. But there is little in the management and leadership research which explores these experiences. A couple of recent studies have extrapolated the skills of managers who are adept at international operations, to build models of 'global literacies' (for example, Rosen 2000). Others put the spotlight on particular leaders who are held up as examples of some kind of global leadership—however that is defined (for example, Kets de Vries and Florent-Treacy (1999) and Trompenaars and Hampden-Turner 2001).

Our research set out to explore how leaders were dealing with difference and how they were reflecting in their approaches to leadership their own range of experiences. The main data for this book were interviews with leaders—CEOs, Managing Directors, General Managers and others with responsibilities for managing business units—which specifically focused on leadership of diversity.

We chose a sample of thirty Australian leaders who, through our processes of selection, were identified as being thoughtful and reflective about these issues. Half of the sample were Australian-born and half born overseas, in Europe, India, Malaysia, China, Korea and elsewhere in the Asian region. A focus of our interest was the experience of crossing borders: geographical and cultural, as well as economic and psychological; of 'outsiders' coming in and 'insiders' going out.

Consistent with the general principle that qualitative research is more appropriate at the exploratory, hypothesis-developing stages of research, we used interviews and thematic analysis to draw insights from our sample. We quote extensively from our thirty interviewees. This is not because we believe they offer a single truth, nor because we take their statements at face value as the facts of the situation. Rather we are interested in reflecting a multi-layered and shifting set of interpretations about the challenges of working across borders and with multicultural workforces. The raw data of the quotes are used to tease out ways of thinking and acting, illustrating the nuances and ambiguities of interpretation. What most interests us is how leaders use and work with their past experiences to reach an understanding, often implicit rather than conscious, about their approach to leadership and how they work with difference.

We have been particularly interested to take the smaller scale of people's experiences with difference and with crossing borders and to see what they made of it in later leadership roles. This has necessitated that we go back to leaders' childhoods and growing-up years where, we argue, powerful templates are formed about how one meets difference: open, engaged and curious, or apprehensive, rigid and fearful. Drawing on Graham Little's (1992) idea that we 'make use' of our childhoods in the service of both identity and ideology, we explore how leaders make a connection between childhood and leadership experiences. Chapters 2 and 3 specifically address how and why childhoods matter.

In Chapter 4 we tease out the features of the leadership that emerge from crossing a variety of borders. While not holding up our sample as exemplars of a bold new approach to leadership, we suggest that it is important to show how these leaders use or infuse their border-crossing experiences in their leadership practices. They are particularly tuned in to a different kind of data and remain, as leaders, more attuned, reflective and flexible. They are also more strategic, in their capacity to step back from the accepted norms of their workplace culture and take a longer and wider perspective. This may be because their identity has multiple roots and some are used to being on the edge or voicing a different perspective. Overall though, the look of this leadership is more subtle and tactical than out-front and grandiose.

Chapter 5 draws on leaders' experiences to map out the continuing pressures to assimilate to a dominant business culture. This chapter introduces a range of research on managers who come from 'minority' backgrounds—their experiences of working across several cultures and the strategies they use to manage multiple value sets and identities. In the later chapters of the book we move from our reliance on interview data to draw in wider contemporary literature on leadership, and specifically work that focuses on global leadership. We have supplemented our findings with those from other researchers examining related phenomena, such as the experience of being a bicultural manager. We use concepts from postmodern theory to reframe a leader strategy of adopting multiple and sometimes contradictory positions about identity and belonging.

In Chapters 6 and 7 we move to the bigger context in which leadership takes place. In this section we discuss the historical, cultural and economic reasons for the entrenchment of a traditional approach to leadership. We introduce the broader structural factors which constrain different approaches to leadership, showing that leadership is rarely a matter of individual discretion. We offer the outlines of a theory of leadership which places personal histories back within the context of study.

The ground underneath leadership has shifted dramatically over the past two or so decades. The tasks of corporate leadership have also changed radically—the issues being considered, the breadth of contextual factors, the roles and responsibilities expected. Borders, cultures and nationalities have changed, but they haven't disappeared as many predicted. All of these changes mean that the old paths are no longer the best apprenticeship to leadership.

Yet if we turn to the study of leaders, the focus and the findings seem lodged in a time-warp in which leaders are still perceived as being great men, expected to turn out heroic performances and deliver feats of transformation.

Our work argues, in contrast, that much new work in leadership is going on in organisations in response to these challenges, but to understand it we need to look in different places and from a different set of perspectives. We also need to analyse the systemic pressures on leaders to censor their differences, to conform, adapt and follow in the footsteps of those who have gone before, rather than adopt radically different leadership directions and postures. Our 'anti-heroes', and their experiences before assuming leadership roles, have much to tell us about leading in a world of difference.

The roots of leadership: childhood and the origins of alternative leadership styles

Are people born to lead? Proud parents might claim their child is 'a born leader'. Biographers of military, political and business leaders sometimes point to 'natural' leadership abilities. The 'nature' or 'nurture' debate in psychology has been passionate and controversial: to what extent are our capacities innate, and to what extent are they the product of our upbringing, experiences and environment?

In business and management literature and research there have been waves of theory about leadership and its origins. But when management education really took hold in the 1950s and 1960s it tended to entrench the view that leadership could be taught—that leaders were made in career, and by organisations, rather than shaped by earlier life experiences. Large organisations in most Western industrialised nations embraced the view emerging from American business and business schools that leadership careers were the culmination of logical planning and organisational orchestration—with a bit of individual aptitude thrown in. They invested heavily in leadership development programs and career-path planning in order to capture expected organisational benefits.

This emphasis on education and planned career development has left a tendency to conceptualise leadership as a performance that the individual delivers, within the organisational context: a performance that is largely unconnected to personal history or character.

Our research shows, however, that backgrounds and personal histories cannot be ignored. Values and habits learned from family; major changes in schooling; landmark circumstances like a parent's death or even moving to a new place—all these life events shape the way in which individuals interact with the world, including the world of work.

This should not be surprising; common sense suggests it would be so. And yet there is little in the management literature which acknowledges links between childhood and later organisational life. Our work demonstrates the vitality of those links by uncovering the personal stories of thirty successful leaders in large Australian corporations. It re-attaches the childhoods and early experiences of senior business people to their evolving organisational lives. It reconnects the private with the public.

It is important to stress that we are not proposing an essentialist argument that puts leadership ability in place (or not) at an early age. Nor do we argue that this is immutable. Clearly one's values and propensities continue to be shaped and developed throughout life. Leadership skills can be encouraged and developed by organisations, just as they can be nurtured, or crushed, in families or in schools. What we do maintain is that to ignore the path by which people arrive at their positions of leadership is to seriously limit the insights to be gained. To ignore personal history is as dangerous as to ignore national history or cultural history in understanding who we are, how we operate and how we might grow.

Furthermore, in thinking about the sorts of leadership qualities which might be required as the world, especially the business world, continues to become globalised, we may find that backgrounds and early experiences become more relevant rather than less. As leaders and managers are 'cut loose' from attachments of family and place—whether operating on-line in virtual business networks or operating globally in multinational organisations—the baggage they carry with them in their heads may be of even greater significance. In the absence of regular physical contact with a home base, with its anchoring habits and norms, it is possible that ways of doing things and thinking about things which were laid down earlier in life will fill the vacuum.

Some studies of expatriate behaviour, and of people working in transcultural teams and organisations, do include 'life experiences' as well as organisational training as significant determinants of success (see Hambrick et al. 1994). A recent study of three British corporate leaders (Kets de Vries and Florent-Treacy 1999) illustrates connections between early family experiences and later corporate styles. For example, Sir Richard Branson, head of the Virgin empire, describes 'very stable environment, a very happy, loving supportive background. My parents have equally wanted me to stand on my own two feet.' Literally, as it turns out. He describes his earliest memory as being in a car in the country at about the age of six: 'My mother shoved me out the door at about six at night and said "make your own way back" ... I ended up at a neighbouring farmhouse'. His mother was the entrepreneurially minded parent: 'she never sits still ... always coming up with another mad idea, another new project. ... I must admit that if I ring up, I always ask for Dad first'. His mum was a BA air stewardess who sent him a photo of herself in uniform, inscribed: 'From an old virgin to a new Virgin, love, your mother'.

It is not just that these snippets of childhood—albeit selected and recreated through the adult CEO's eyes—make interesting stories. They also provide potent clues to the continuing impetus for a leadership career: a mother who demanded, and rewarded, risk-taking; a father who provided sufficient support and love for it to turn out all right in the end.

Various schools of psychology emphasise the central significance of early family relationships in the development of attributes such as trust and a capacity for intimacy and creativity. Research on the origins of prejudice, for example, shows the importance of parental influence in the development of world views about 'them' and 'us', in the development of coping strategies and ways of handling anxiety and discomfort. What is clear is that these basic orientations take root relatively early in our lives (Adorno et al. 1950; Allport 1954).

In *The Leadership Factor* (1988: 34–5), John Kotter describes the origins of the characteristics required to provide effective leadership. He lists the four 'origins': inborn capacity, early childhood, formal education and career experiences. These origins contribute to eight 'personal requirements'. The first three origins are particularly strong contributors to the first three requirements: motivation (for leadership), personal values, and abilities and skills. The fourth origin (career experience) more strongly shapes the last three requirements: reputation and track record, relationships in the firm and industry, and organisational knowledge. Overall, Kotter concludes that to 'account for why [leaders] were able to do what they did . . . it was necessary to trace their experience from birth, through childhood and education and on into their careers. It was the accumulative effect of those many experiences that gave them the assets needed for leadership'.

Writing about educational leaders, Peter Gronn also points out the connection between 'preparatory socialization processes and experiences' and later leadership qualities, styles and effectiveness: 'It is in this formative period, from infancy to early adulthood, that the scaffolding of a character structure . . . is erected' (1999: 34). Gronn suggests that the 'core aspects' of leadership character determined by these antecedent experiences include a conception of self and identity, a preferred working style and an outlook or set of values.

Thomas and Gabarro's study of senior executives from American minority groups shows that early experiences—family, parental models and schooling—are important ingredients of later success (1999: 117). Their discussions with senior minority executives revealed that prior experiences of dealing with racism or prejudice, and in some cases exposure to the consciousness-raising activities of activists, had enabled them to develop 'confidence in their ability to effectively perform and work with whites. In addition, they gained comfort and experience with being bicultural'. The authors show that working in a predominantly white domain taught high-achieving minority executives how to work around obstacles (people and things). They also tended to develop strong rapport with supportive mentors and, interestingly, they adapted their own senses of racial identity according to the context they were in (from merging/passing through to stronger espousal of racial identity). Critically, these experiences left a legacy not just of professional competence but also of personal confidence—'a distinct pattern of early experiences that enabled minority executives to build on their professional foundation, despite many opportunities to become discouraged, especially by the slow take-off of their careers relative to white executives' (1999: 93–119).

Where do leaders come from? Family structure and early experiences

In our research we focused on two samples of leaders. First there was a sample of Australian leaders of mainstream corporations, mostly born here or in similarly Anglo-Celtic countries such as New Zealand, who were known to be interested in issues relating to the management of diverse workplaces. Half our sample fell into this category. These we call the apparent 'insiders'.

The other half of the sample consisted of leaders of mainstream corporations who were born or raised elsewhere, mostly in non-English-speaking countries. These we call the apparent 'outsiders'. Unlike the self-made migrant enterprise success stories, of which there are many, migrant corporate leaders from non-English-speaking backgrounds who have risen up the ranks to the top of mainstream corporations in Australia remain a relatively rare breed. In the overall Australian business scene, as in the literature on entrepreneurship generally, there is a disproportionate representation of people who are immigrants. This phenomenon—of people mobilised to great economic achievement by the disadvantage of their dislocation—is a fascinating and important contribution to the study of leadership. But it is not our focus here. We were precisely interested in the experience of 'outsiders' who have made their way to leadership through the twists and turns of traditional large corporate workplaces.

Moreover, while there is great value in charting the experiences of those who have struggled against outsider status (see for example Hawthorne 1988; Cope and Kalantzis 2000), our focus has not been on assessing how these individuals have 'made it against the odds' into positions of leadership. Rather, our work explores and describes the ways in which their leadership reflects their own experiences.

Identifying people for this part of our sample was a challenging task. The number of individuals fitting this profile is still small in corporate Australia. Furthermore, there is no organisation that registers or collates such information. We worked through multiple and diverse contacts, doing a lot of legwork and phone calling, in order to identify 'outsider' leaders for our sample. Another explanation for their elusiveness emerged from our interviews: our 'outsider' leaders are ambivalent about their difference—when, whether and where to celebrate it. The multiple reasons for the elusiveness and invisibility of outsider leaders is discussed in more detail in Chapter 5. Detailed information about the research process itself may be found in the Appendix.

Insiders—moving out

Firstly the apparent insiders. This half of our sample looked conventional: they were Anglo-Celtic men (mostly) and women who had worked their ways up to the top echelons of large corporations. On the surface, they were the successful insiders. But it was fascinating to discover that most had emerged from family environments in which they felt different or where there was significant dysfunction. That is, there had been considerable disruption or major family events that catapulted leaders from stability to instability.

Absent fathers
More than half of the men had grown up without strong father identification. Their fathers had either died when they were young, or had been away a lot on business, or were emotionally withdrawn from family life. Some of our insider leaders simply did not relate to disconnected or remote fathers. Others, coming later in the birth order, lacked the close attention from father that a first-born son often experiences.

This meant that mothers often played a larger role in their lives, and/or they found other mentors. Consequently, they experienced less of the traditional 'masculine' gender role modelling—with its hierarchical, competitive emphases—and correspondingly more of the female influence, stressing relationships and personal inter-actions. One man described his upbringing in a particularly female environment: 'My father had a few strokes and was pretty wrapped up in his own world. So my mother and aunt and grand-mother were important figures in my life . . .'

It was also clear that several of our interviewees found individual ways of forging identity which fostered independence and flexi-bility. This is how a very senior executive talked about the death of both his parents in an air crash in Africa. It had been his parents' first trip overseas to visit a family member. He was twenty-four, well past the childhood formative years, but nevertheless this event was a turning-point in his young adult life and career:

> That experience is part of the fabric of my [interest in] diversity because I had only been married a year and we had to take in and bring up my youngest brother who was only fourteen. When it happened, I had to fly to Rhodesia to deal with things—I hadn't a clue but I waded in. It took eight weeks to sort things out . . . But it's all part of the web that's spun for you and it's part of that adaptability. Then you know how and can apply it in other contexts. To survive in organisations, especially at executive level, that adaptability comes into play all the time.

This was a man who had grown up in a small coal-mining town in the UK, and was the first in his family to go to university. In fact he had always pushed boundaries, with his mother's encouragement: 'I had a great home life but it was too small, I could see that there were other things to be done'. He was one of a number of male interviewees who cited their mothers as the major influence on their lives.

Another interviewee told this story:

> My father had to retire when I was at school because he was injured in a car accident. He wanted all of my mother's time, he was totally obsessed with being ill and stopped her working . . . he couldn't accept that she should spend time with us. So my younger sister and I had to fend for ourselves . . . we became totally independent because we needed to get on and do what we wanted to do. Which is a good thing . . .

In this leadership career, taking many different paths in its early stages including some unusual travel experiences, people outside the family—neighbours, early employers—had provided the significant influences.

In his 1983 book, *Leaders We Deserve*, Alistair Mant describes research showing that sons in families where father was absent for at least two years in childhood developed aptitude scores which looked more like those of intelligent young women. Those with fathers who were present tended to show the typical male bias towards mathematics. Absence of a strong fatherly influence can create, or leave, a space that sets some men free to become more 'creative', or less constrained to adopt conservative forms of masculinity.

In the political sphere, former US President Bill Clinton and UK Prime Minister Tony Blair are described sometimes as 'third way' leaders. By 'third way' is meant a leadership that 'escapes standard constraints' and is based on imagining 'transforming' solutions rather than the transactional deal-making of other leader styles (Little 1999). One of the interesting things about Clinton and Blair is that both had childhoods characterised, one way or another, by insecure father identification. The leadership style of these two men contrasts strongly with that of President George W. Bush, whose middle initial is apparently all that separates him from his father and mentor, former President George Bush senior. George W. Bush favours the more traditional tough-minded conservatism that is an extension of his father's style.

By contrast, the absence of an active father role model may allow sons to find a different masculine path, a sense of themselves as men that is neither as traditional or constraining. It can allow space for sons to be more fully themselves, accommodating or developing aspects of personality which may be more commonly associated with traditionally feminine strengths. This may include, for example, a greater emphasis on interpersonal relationships.

The work of psychologists such as Carol Gilligan (1982), Jean Baker Miller (1986) and Belenky and her colleagues (1986) shows that 'connection' is a central value in the socialisation of young women. They show how from very early childhood, women tend to put a high value on maintaining relationships and minimising hurt. This then plays out in adult moral systems and learning styles, but has been routinely devalued in models which privilege traditional male values such as upholding abstract logic and maintaining hierarchy.

The distinction between 'binary' and 'ternary' leaders which Alistair Mant introduced in *Leaders We Deserve* was picked up again in his later book *Intelligent Leadership* (1997). The binary leader is typically the fight/flight, winner/loser, all or nothing power type. The ternary leader has less interest in personal power, preferring to exercise authority rather than power. The ternary leader incorporates an additional dimension, a 'third corner', which consists of a higher goal or value, from which this leader derives his or her sense of authority or purpose. Mant argues that Clinton and Blair fall into this ternary group.

Relationships, however, are not necessarily the most important thing for the ternary leader. Indeed ternary leaders often are, or see themselves, as 'outsiders'. Moreover, while people may be predisposed by background factors to one or other position primarily, these may not be rigidly fixed; they may move from one mode to another depending on circumstances or contexts. But people in ternary mode handle ambiguity and contradiction well. As Graham Little put it: 'the central paradox remains being empowered by leaders who lead without putting you down. Ternary leaders have the personalities to handle such contradictions, are so little fussed about themselves, their personality, they are free to respond as they will' (1999: 16).

In an early study entitled *Society Without the Father* (1963), Mitscherlich pursued the concept of fatherlessness in the context of social changes in the twentieth century. He was interested in the individual and social consequences of absent or invisible fathers, as well as 'the disappearance of the father imago so closely associated with the roots of our civilization, and of the paternal instructive function . . . [which] is the result of historical processes and is accompanied by a revolution in values'. Connecting with the classic studies by David Riesman (1961), Mitscherlich examines what happens when societies progressively lose or abandon systems of 'direct and immediate instruction in practical life under the paternal eye'. Among the consequences are the disappearance of 'maturity' as a 'collectively acknowledged aim' and its replacement with shorter-term goals, such as keeping up with contemporaries.

Also, 'that highly important thing, the way in which his father gained his livelihood, ceased to be visible to the child' and the father then makes his appearance in the child's world as a terror-striking figure or a figure of fun—either way distant (1969: 141–50).

While there may be profound negative consequences associated with this absence of strong paternal traditions in society and the family, Mitscherlich argued that one way people learn to orient themselves is via the peer group and a different set of identifications through work. What our research is suggesting is that individuals who come at leadership via a different set of family circumstances and experiences may indeed bring a different repertoire of approaches to leadership—more concerned with connections with others, less reliant on traditional paternalistic hierarchy. We see that changes in family structures do have consequences for the values and styles of adult leaders.

Birth order

Leadership studies have traditionally indicated a preponderance of first-born sons in the ranks of leaders in politics, business and society (see for example Mant's discussion: 1983: 45). Studies of women political leaders confirm that an extraordinarily high proportion of women in political office consists of first-borns, commonly from all-girl families. Particularly if they don't have any brothers, these women experience a range of influences, including paternal attention and high aspirations, that produce leadership motivations (Steinberg undated).

Yet our work, as well as other more recent research, draws attention to the possibility of different roots of leadership, without the strong paternal identification of the first-born. Indeed we have found that there may be a 'positive' impact of absent or 'distant' fathers. In addition, there were two other fascinating features of our sample of insider Anglo-Celtic leaders.

Firstly, most of our interviewees came from larger families. Of the fifteen, only one was an only child, while eight came from families with four or more children. Three were from three-child families and three from two-child families, yielding an average of close to four children per family. By contrast, in the general

Australian population, only 5 per cent of families have four or more children.

This finding suggests something about boundaries. The larger the family, the more human boundaries there are to 'negotiate', the more one might learn about relationships—the complexities and the subtleties—and about being flexible. While large families might produce fierce attachments to one's own territory, nevertheless the realities of living with several others test those attachments on a daily basis.

Secondly, the majority of leaders in our 'insider' Anglo-Celtic sample came later in the birth order rather than being the eldest. Nine of the ten male interviewees were further down in birth order—third of four, fourth of six, sixth of seven and so on. This suggests that second and subsequent children might become different sorts of leader—more naturally democratic perhaps. As Alistair Mant (1983) notes, subsequent children in a family have a vested interest in fairness, in fair play and a fair go for all. This links to qualities such as diversity-mindedness, to an empathy with people who lack power, an ability to negotiate pathways, a desire to see fair play in organisations.

Research shows that the bigger the family—the more children there are—the more likely is the first-born to excel intellectually. In addition, first-borns tend to be both bossy and dutiful, hankering after the absolute parental attention they once had. Alistair Mant claims that first-borns are more likely to be binary types, with a bi-polar world view, whereas second and subsequent children are more likely to be ternary in orientation. Again, they may be seen as natural democrats, with a vested interest in fair play. These are the filters through which they view the world and relationships, personal and organisational. As Mant sums up the issues: 'mothering (or nurturance) and birth order together provide the bedrock upon which personality is built. The foundation cannot specify the edifice that will grow on its site, but it limits the kind of structure that is possible. It characterizes the quality of leading and of following that an individual will be capable of and impelled towards' (1983: 55).

Graham Little's discussion of Mant's work expresses the impact on leadership of birth order and family structures in this way:

'Binary leadership is masculine and comes naturally to older brothers, and bosses. Ternary leadership comes naturally to younger brothers, because it's nimble, inventive, critical and creative ... Women are honorary younger brothers: outsiders and "emergent" like younger brothers, where older brothers are insiders who have been "anointed". The leadership world is divided between binary older brothers and ternary *nths*, that is, the rest; between the establishment and all of us who have had the good fortune to grow up outsiders' (1999: 15).

In summary, one's position in the family affects ideas about one's place in the world and about working with others. Our subjects from large families had developed finely honed powers of observation, awareness of differences, of nuances. Their childhoods provided opportunities to practise—not necessarily consciously—empathy, negotiation skills, appropriate assertion skills, the importance of good timing and so on. Several also mentioned their sense of 'outsiderness', of feeling a bit detached from the hurly-burly of large family life.

So paradoxically we have insiders who often feel like outsiders and go on to lead organisations in ways which might benefit from their insider's operational skills and their outsider's observational skills. Our research shows that individuals who come at leadership via a different set of family circumstances and experiences may indeed bring a different repertoire of approaches to leadership—more concerned with connections with others, less reliant on traditional paternal hierarchy.

Adolescence, schooling, migration

Another set of influences which interviewees experienced in their adolescent years has been touched upon in some of the preceding stories. These influences are connected with school experiences and/or with movement or migration. In general terms, they cluster around change or variety in physical boundaries, especially during adolescence.

Several of our interviewees had changed countries or changed schools, in some cases several times, exposing them to foreignness and difference and creating a need for adaptability. Mostly, and with the benefit of hindsight, this was experienced as an enormously positive expanding of outlook and possibility, instilling confidence about moving and an appetite for cultural differences that became a major plank of identity. The following is a Europe-born CEO speaking:

> I was lucky enough to get a scholarship to the US and spent a year in a US high school. That was a wonderful experience. It has changed my outlook on life completely. At that time there were enormous differences in living standards, technologies and lifestyles . . . And I became very interested in other countries and after I finished university I went to Sweden for a few years, Switzerland, back to the States, Germany . . . So I've really always considered myself an internationalist. I was interested in languages . . . had business dealings in many parts of the world. I'd always seen that as very rewarding and I liked doing it . . . It has really been my formative years that have been very decisive for this outlook.

Another interviewee spent his childhood moving around remote north-west Australia. His father was a primary school teacher and often his was the only white family in predominantly Aboriginal communities. This created the experience of being an outsider within Australia, of being the one who was different. It was a very positive experience and one through which he made many Aboriginal friends. His father also provided a strong role model in his work in these remote communities, instilling in the son a lifelong commitment to social justice.

For some others in our sample, migration did not feel like a positive experience at the time: being different at a new school can bring particular agonies to a child, and especially in adolescence. But it resulted in an empathy later with others experiencing difference, or experiencing the difficulties of 'outsider' status. As another CEO described:

> I was born in the UK but my mother was Australian, my father English. When I was eight we all moved back to Australia and that's interesting, it's another diversity issue—coming back here I was perceived by the kids at primary school as an English person. There were lots of other nationalities too—Greeks, Italians, Yugoslavs—but you're initially excluded and you have to fight to be included . . .

Several interviewees deliberately extended the boundaries themselves—pushing outwards—as in the story of the son of a coalminer told earlier: he had moved to university away from his home town and then taken a teaching position in France while still a student. Others of our interviewees had actively rebelled: for example, against established patterns in the family. One woman had run off interstate at the age of eighteen and married her boyfriend who was in the army. She was escaping what she felt were constraining and rather 'boring' expectations held about her likely career and life prospects. Although the experience had been far from positive—she experienced dislocation, loneliness, unemployment and subsequent divorce—she had coped with adversity and disadvantage, then re-trained as a psychologist. She believed that all this had fed practical and intuitive understanding of many problems which arose in later management positions, especially in dealing with the sort of issues which come under the banner of diversity management. In another example, a South African interviewee had rebelled against the dominant apartheid politics of his time. His experiences of growing up in South Africa, including compulsory military service and institutionalised racism, clearly provided a formative backdrop for his adult views on how differences are managed in the workplace.

English playwright and actor Steven Berkoff has been quoted as saying: 'Anyone with anything to contribute has to feel an outsider because of the entrenched establishment. Anyone of any quality feels an outsider' (*Sunday Age*, 26 September 1999). Why might the experience of being an outsider at some time add to one's capacity to 'contribute'? At a mundane level we know that often outsiders can 'see' things—patterns, problems, possible solutions—which those on the inside cannot. This is partly due to cognitive effects of perception and sense-making (Weick 1995). When we are surrounded by familiar circumstances our assumptions override our capacity to accurately read a situation. The insider will simply see 'business as usual', while the outsider will say 'this looks odd' or 'this might be a problem'. This sharpened perception of outsiders was the phenomenon noted in *Trials at the Top* (Sinclair 1994), where the homogeneity of senior levels of Australian companies was overwhelmingly obvious to American executives hired in to lead those companies, but was not obvious to the locals.

Culture moulds our views in ways we rarely notice. Research by Robert Nisbett and his colleagues provides a powerful demonstration of this phenomenon (reported in Adler 2000). The researchers found that American students focus on the largest object in a picture while the Japanese and Koreans students pay more attention to the context and the apparent incidentals. Further, in their reasoning and reaction to new or contradictory information, US students argue more strongly for their original position while the East Asian students accommodate ambiguity in their hypotheses. This work builds on a body of research on cross-cultural differences (notably Geert Hofstede 1980; 1991) and the effects of those differences in shaping not only our world views but also much more specific matters of work orientation, strengths and weaknesses. It shows that our cultural inheritance does, at a deep and unconscious level, shape what we take in and how we proceed. The experience of being a border-crosser, shared by many in our sample, brings new and sometimes startling insights into things taken for granted within the comfort of cultural stasis. It is likely to make visible phenomena that may not be visible to those brought up in a more monocultural environment or without the challenges brought about by cross-border experiences.

People who have thrust themselves, or been thrust by circumstances, into challenging situations without their normal supports often learn new things about themselves. Howard Gardner (1984; 1993) says that highly disruptive experiences of being an outsider can sharpen intelligences, particularly creative intelligence. It does this by throwing people back on their own resources and giving them the experience of operating without approval of others, being more self-sufficient in terms of esteem and identity needs. It is commonly observed that qualities of creativity and performances of great artistry and invention are often forged from trauma and suffering.

The experience of being an outsider also has an impact politically. Not being an insider gives one an experience of disadvantage and makes mechanisms of systemic discrimination more real and observable. This can often put in place an enduring identification with people who are disadvantaged on the basis of their difference.

A central task of adolescence, according to theorists such as Erikson, is identity formation (1968). For a number of our interviewees, events in adolescence critically shaped their developing views of self and how different others would be regarded—as threats or as potentially deserving of respect. Adolescence is known as a time when peer group affiliation is critical, but some of our interviewees were deprived of the comfort of easy conformity. One interviewee describes how his father's job as a psychiatric nurse in a small Queensland country town influenced his view of others:

> My father had a genuine interest in people. He worked with alcoholic patients and would often bring them home. My friends used to say, 'You've got looneys at your house', but my Dad thought that was an important part of their rehabilitation—to bring them home . . . sometimes you'd feel embarrassed but as I got a bit older and more mature, I obviously thought that was a very positive thing.

All these stories and experiences have in common the changing of physical boundaries and the extending of emotional boundaries at a time when identity is being formed. They have equipped people to be flexible and resilient. The challenge of developing new relationships in new places has fine-tuned their interpersonal skills and pushed them, often uncomfortably at the time, into experiences which now stand them in good stead for the exercise of leadership in a changing world.

Outsiders—moving in

The second half of our sample consisted of leaders who had been born in other countries, mostly non-English-speaking countries. These are therefore 'real' outsiders in the Australian corporate context, as opposed to interviewees in our 'insider' sample above who had sometimes felt like outsiders. The people in the second part of our sample had risen to the most senior ranks in mainstream companies in Australia, overcoming hurdles of language, culture and customs. Many had made their way alone, without the comfort of family to cushion some of life's rougher episodes.

Indeed many of these 'outsider' leaders had extraordinary stories to tell about their upbringings, about dramatic changes and hardships endured. Their families had often had to start again from nothing, stripped of history, of language, of kinships, of livelihoods. Out of these experiences we see qualities of resilience, determination and courage as well as the desire to succeed and to make a difference. They had developed essentially optimistic outlooks on life, with an abiding sense that individual effort can overcome adversity through ability, tenacity and hard work.

At the same time it was clear that experiences of hardship in such transitions are contextual. For a number of our interviewees, the conditions from which they came were so horrendous that Australia was genuinely a 'country of great promise' by comparison. Immediate post-war immigrants felt 'wanted' here, with bipartisan political support for the immigration program, and they enjoyed reasonably high levels of popular support. Sir Arvi Parbo, who migrated from Estonia in 1949 and went on to become Chief Executive and later Chairman of Western Mining Corporation, described his experience:

> We were eager to leave war-torn Europe, to get away from the unpleasant happenings of its recent past, the then sad present, and the unpromising looking future. We wanted the chance to start our lives again in a country where there was freedom, the opportunity to improve ourselves through our efforts, and minimum interferences with our ability to do so. Australia, to us, looked like such a country. We did not expect anything to be given to us. Whatever problems we might have settling in were, to us, not worth considering compared with the opportunities ahead.

Some of our interviewees found they were the only Asians or Indians in their local areas and were therefore 'special' or 'exotic'. They were often treated with fond curiosity, 'adopted' by locals and included in local rituals. Their assimilation was facilitated by this environment and most shared a migrant aspiration of 'trying to fit in'.

Individual experiences of stereotyping and discrimination were counterbalanced to some degree within a generally supportive climate. It didn't mean that there was no discrimination, but migrants were not attacked as taking jobs earmarked for Australians, nor feared as the first trickle in a flood of invaders set to decimate a precarious Anglo-Australian identity—as was to happen later. Discrimination and racism were also seen as relative: a number of our leaders mentioned that, compared with some other countries, Australia 'all in all would be the least discriminatory country, compared to say France or Germany'.

Migrants arriving in Australia from the late 1970s onwards experienced a very different climate. Immigration was to become highly politicised, and migrants from some countries and regions were less welcome than others. The White Australia policy, which had originated in 1901, was not finally dismantled until 1973, and migrants from Asian and Indian regions on the whole continue to experience far more distrust and discrimination than their European counterparts.

It must be said, however, that the group that has experienced the most institutionalised and widespread discrimination in Australia is not a migrant group at all but indigenous Australians. Although we sought to identify indigenous corporate leaders for our sample we were unsuccessful. This is an important finding in itself. The experiences of indigenous leaders has become the subject of another research project.

It is also important to make the point that migrant experiences are various. There is not one path to 'making it' but many. There is a clear hierarchy of different immigrant groups, some types of minority status enjoying attention as special or exotic, others attracting enmity and pervasive discrimination. This hierarchy is no secret; it is widely commented on and a source of profound concern for many of our interviewees. It has little to do with the individual characteristics of the immigrant. The hierarchy is shaped by historical patterns of racism and colonisation as well as by contemporary government policies and economic conditions.

As with the 'insider' leaders from mainstream backgrounds described earlier, we have identified a number of important childhood influences which characterise these migrant journeys to leadership and which have shaped the styles of leadership they have evolved. Again, the experiences can be summed up as border-crossing. However, the borders for this outsider sample include geographical, cultural, linguistic and socio-economic borders. Their border-crossing experience has promoted openness to difference and change. These people find that they can adapt and 'belong' in multiple places, their identity not solely defined by their place of birth. Border-crossing has promoted sensitivity to differences—large and overt differences as well as small and subtle differences. Their success is partially attributable to their skills in reading people and situations and adapting appropriately.

Families and parental influence

The early experiences of family and upbringing were as important for 'born offshore' leaders as for our 'born local' interviewees—perhaps more so.

Interestingly, as with the 'locals' these overseas-born leaders were rarely first-borns. They were more often second or later in birth order, and larger families were common. Of the fifteen overseas-born leaders, twelve were second or later born and seven were from families with four or more children. In general they came from larger families, with the average number of siblings being 3.9. As we noted earlier, only 5 per cent of families in the general Australian population have four or more children and only 1.3 per cent have five or more.

As we also pointed out earlier, being a second or later-born child is a fundamentally different experience from being first-born, when parental expectations can create strong pressures to achieve. Being a first-born might also encourage inflated views of one's centrality, perhaps retained by those who remain only children but usually deflated for those who have to cope with the arrival of subsequent sibling rivals! Coming second or third in largish families builds particular skills in two obvious ways. First, parental attention cannot be assumed as it can for first-borns—it has to be earned and shared. Later-borns cannot rely on their position in the family to be respected and heard and they don't have the vested interest in hierarchy that first-born children have. This potential negative becomes a positive, as later-borns are not subject to the same pressure to reproduce the paternal model of leadership, and they often have more space and freedom to find their own path, including their own path to leadership.

The second important experience for later-born children is that they have to work with and around siblings. As we discussed earlier, this experience of having to 'fit in' and find a place in a larger family promotes the development of interpersonal skills, of being sensitive to others and learning how to negotiate to get what one needs. They have to develop alliances and work out how to compete without permanently alienating others. Listening to and learning from siblings become critical skills. Negotiating a place for oneself, rather than assuming one's place, becomes a primary developmental task. This in turn lays the foundation for the listening and learning capabilities of the open-minded leader.

In our overseas-born sample, paternal influences are strong but often mitigated by the changing circumstances of mobile lives. This group of leaders drew many lessons from fathers, especially about the value of hard work, education and transcending difficulties. In a number of cases their fathers had had to re-train in altogether different occupations, finding new dimensions of themselves. In one case the transition was from the military to teaching, in another it was from being a priest, then a teacher and soldier, and finally a doctor turned psychiatrist very late in life. These examples are important because they model openness, the positive possibilities in change, of personal growth. It was the models of fathers and mothers adapting to new circumstances that mattered. One interviewee summed up:

> I never thought I can't achieve or reach. Maybe this was driven by my father. He was very confident. And he's had much higher stumbling blocks than I have had to overcome—from village to boat to no money in Australia. Huge.

Parents gave these leaders the sense that they could achieve, albeit via pathways which were not necessarily linear or rigidly prescribed: 'they conveyed that I had the ability to be a success. They gave me self-esteem and optimism'.

Experiences of and exposure to multiple cultures
Many of the childhoods of these leaders included experiences of exposure to multiple cultures along with an early sensitivity to the importance of subtle differences. Some of their families were extra-

ordinarily international in their history and outlook. In Chapter 1 we described the rich and diverse childhood experiences of our Portuguese-Chinese leader, moving from multicultural Shanghai to cosmopolitan Hong Kong and thence to a small country town in rural New South Wales.

Several interviewees had come from Malaysia: a country with three major cultural/religious/linguistic strands, Malay, Chinese and Indian, with an additional touch of British colonial heritage remaining in its formal structures and processes. Another interviewee was born in England, spent his first five years in Austria and then moved to New Zealand. This experience left a lasting 'hunger for foreign languages and different places', evidenced by the fact that during his adolescence he would 'go out to the airport to watch the planes depart', imagining he was on them. On graduating he sought the first opportunity he could to get back to Europe, fronting up to the foreign embassies to see whether he could obtain a position with a European company.

As we have already noted, this sort of exposure to multiple cultures in childhood and adolescence creates individuals who, even if they hanker for stability and predictability in their lives, never really lose their sense of other possibilities or their predisposition to be open to new people and new situations.

Being a newcomer or an outsider

For many of our interviewees, school was a tough but formative experience where, with a combination of huge determination, ability and hard work, obstacles like not speaking English were overcome. One described arriving as part of a 'penniless migrant family':

> I went to school, so I had to speak English. I brought with me 'Three Blind Mice' and 'yes' and 'no' . . . Children are very cruel and one learns very quickly . . . I was the only migrant at my school.. but I won the English prize there in my final year. I had a wonderful English teacher and I showed them.

In several cases, interviewees excelled at maths and sciences, subjects in which English language fluency wasn't such an obstacle. Over three years in a very large Queensland school, one moved from being fifty-sixth to fourth in the seventy-eight children of his year. Another leader from an Italian background recalls the kinds of experiences of migrant children in the 1950s:

> It was not harrowing at all except for one teacher with no patience, where it was humiliating and embarrassing a couple of times when he'd scream at me and say, 'That's your problem, tough luck, you shouldn't have gone back to Italy', things like that. But that's the only thing I can remember as a culture clash. The other was on the soccer field, the Italians are very passionate about playing soccer. I remember my first game in Australia and scoring a goal in a friendly game and going crazy like the Italians do when they score, and everyone's looking at me saying, 'Who's this wog?'

While those from European backgrounds may have experienced prejudice at this time, the Asian and Indian-born leaders in our sample were often the only non-white children in their Australian school environments. Sometimes this was experienced as a sense of 'specialness', but instances of negative stereotyping, prejudice and discrimination during schooling were common. A number came from sophisticated school environments and a multilingual home country population to much more basic schools in Australia, yet it was they who were assumed to be 'backward'.

Experiences of racism and prejudice fuelled several things. For many, it put in place an overwhelming determination to belong, which is still being manifested in their organisational and leadership lives (see later chapters). It also fuelled a determination to succeed, to prove themselves 'even better'. Being different or singled out as children put in place life-long habits of achieving in order to overcome tokenism:

> I went through primary school in the 1960s in a state school in a well-to-do area. There was a lot of racism, a lot. You were made to feel different. Not physical on the whole but all the taunts, 'Ching, chong, Chinaman', that sort of stuff. I felt it. Seeing myself as Australian, then finding myself with a whole bunch of kids where I looked different and was made to feel different. Out of that came, one, a strong desire to belong and to be accepted as an Australian. The second thing was to inspire a view that may have already been there—'Well, I'll show the

bastards I'm better than any of them anyway' . . . An element of adversity in most people's lives is a very good thing. I was lucky, I have had adversity in the best possible way.

Another man said:

My father was a very hard worker. If my parents were working six or seven days a week, we saw that. . . . And it has always been part of my style. I do work hard. I was never naturally gifted at sport. I reach a certain level which I am very pleased about, but whereas others reach it by training three days a week, I did it by training five days a week—just to make the team.

In their interviews, some claimed they had not noticed the taunts, or that they'd ignored them, shrugged them off. Yet they recognised that this adult perspective might not reflect accurately the pain of the child's feelings of rejection at the time. Virtually all—some consciously, others intuitively—intensified efforts to succeed and belong as a result of being seen as an outsider. For many of the men in our sample, sport was—and continues to provide—an entree into groups, earning respect and much sought after belonging. Sometimes this was a matter of pursuing the most 'Aussie' of sports. An Italian rejected soccer in favour of rugby and cricket. Another, of Chinese background, developed a passion for machines and cars, assembling a motor bike in his bedroom and running a bike-parts business while at his private school. Other Asian interviewees became passionate swimmers, surfers or even lifesavers, as we saw in Chapter 1. Interest in cricket linked those from countries with a British heritage to the sporting passions of many Australians.

Many developed highly sophisticated social antennae and emotional intelligence skills which were, to some degree, a result of the experiences of being rejected or constantly having to demonstrate one's eligibility for inclusion. Because they could never assume belonging, but had to work to earn it, the social 'radar was always turned on, you become very adaptable, very good at making others feel comfortable'.

Several had experienced discrimination in social situations. As a teenager, one found that he wasn't permitted to accompany his own girlfriend to a debutante ball. While he had no trouble with peer group friendships, or attracting girlfriends, it was the parents —an older generation—who were sometimes opposed: 'doors would close and they [friends] would get into a lot of trouble for seeing me'. Under parental pressure, a local-born mate accompanied the girlfriend to the ball!

People from immigrant backgrounds often developed friendships with other 'outsiders'. One describes an incident when he, an Asian, was not excluded from the local swimming pool, but his Papua New Guinean school friends were. A number of our interviewees were acutely sensitive to the discrimination experienced by blacks in Australia, which they had witnessed but had not felt themselves. One Indian CEO described an incident involving his wife in their early days in Australia. When she wore Western clothes the neighbours thought she was Aboriginal and she was insulted and ignored. When she put on a sari she was exotic and welcomed into homes.

Further down the track, spouses and/or children acted as catalysts for broadening social interactions and networks, many interviewees conveying the impression that it was a 'whole family' effort, that they worked as a team to gain a sense of belonging: 'I try to fully experience the local environment as best I can, rather than restrict myself to an expatriate community. And my wife is particularly good at that. We've been able to do that as a family.'

Inheriting values of hard work and education

It is hard to overplay the emphases on hard work and education in the early lives of our outsider leaders. Many of their fathers had had difficult experiences: sometimes condemned, despite previous education and/or success, to work at menial jobs, putting up with tedious or backbreaking work, working extra-long hours to build up savings or to promote their careers. The following extract is typical:

> My father was an electrician—more educated and skilled than many of the traditional south European migrants. He got a job as a nightshift worker at Unilever. When things broke down, he could fix them and was called on. He moved up quickly to become re-certificated and qualified as an electrician. He was very hardworking and successful. He bought one house then another, did it up at night after the day job and

on weekends, then rented it out. I worked with dad as 'apprentice' from age three!! I used to love that—it was a problem later on in life because my wife had to teach me to have a rest on weekends, not work. Rest was an interesting concept!

Particularly among our Asian-born leaders, hard work is a universal theme and the opportunity to achieve, a privilege. They are motivated either because they had to support themselves or they needed to justify the support of parents:

I've always been ambitious because I come from a poor background and if you're given an opportunity you should make good use of it. That's the way I approach life' . . . so when I got the opportunity to go to a big city at age seventeen to earn my own living, it looked like a challenge and a privilege.

The importance of education is also a strong theme. In some cases, families did not pressure so much as demonstrate a high degree of confidence and support for their children to excel:

Their advice was to work extremely hard to make it in the big world. In that way we have a lot of ambition, to prove that we can do it. I studied hard, when I joined [organisation] I had to prove myself early in my career. I took extra lessons to get my diploma and passed it in record time, in one and a half years where normally it takes three to five years to do it so. While my colleagues were playing mahjong and enjoying themselves I go to my books . . . So I got a bit of a reward there with promotions very quickly. I got to be a branch manager at the tender age of twenty-three.

The leaders we have interviewed—both those we have called the insiders as well as the outsiders—carry into their approaches to management and leadership deep-seated attitudes and orientations substantially shaped by family characteristics, family circumstances, schooling and social experiences. For all of our interviewees, now successful corporate leaders, their experiences have been characterised by the crossing of multiple boundaries, sometimes literal or geographical and often psychological and emotional. Our leaders have drawn personal lessons from those experiences that have affected the style and content of their work lives.

By digging under the surface to expose the roots of leadership we come away with two important messages:

- It is unwise to ignore personal antecedents in seeking to understand the wellsprings of successful leadership.
- Successful leaders have often undergone significantly dislocating experiences in early life which, though tough at the time, have stood them in good stead for navigating corporate life.

These experiences can be usefully summarised as multiple border-crossing—physical, mental and emotional. They have equipped our successful leaders, insiders and outsiders, with skills and aptitudes which have been both literally and figuratively 'the making' of them.

We will turn in the next chapter to charting some specific effects of these early experiences in their pathways to leadership positions.

The routes to leadership: the insiders, the outsiders, multiple pathways

Early influences and experiences have affected the pathways taken by our leaders. The on-going legacies of those formative experiences are carried into a work context. This chapter continues the emphasis on personal histories as we map the paths of 'insiders' and 'outsiders' in early career. It is entitled 'The Routes to Leadership' in order to underline the multiplicity of paths that may be taken and the various border-crossing experiences that shape leadership style.

For the insiders, the focus is on experiences in early career that took interviewees out of the familiar or comfortable and exposed them to different sets of experiences. These, we argue, leave a legacy of ingredients for a new kind of leadership, characterised by openness, trust, flexibility and courage.

Naturally enough, there is considerable variation in the individual experiences and in their effects. There is also variation in the ways in which such experiences are processed and internalised. However, although individual pathways may vary, we found that there were two predominant modalities or orientations, especially to the management of difference and change. Among our insider leaders we found that there was a 'head' path and a 'heart' path.

The second part of the chapter looks at the very different early career experiences of outsiders. These are stories of being highly visible—sometimes exotic, sometimes insulted or marginalised;

being subject to more managerial hurdles; earning belonging through hard work, persistence and exceeding expectations; finding common ground through colonial pasts or sporting interests.

Insiders

For our apparent insiders (that is, people of Anglo-Celtic stock, born here or in similar countries (such as the UK, South Africa, New Zealand), more than half had arrived in their present corporate positions from quite different fields. These varied workplace experiences had extended the range of their social and professional lives. For example, two had commenced their working lives in the Commonwealth Employment Service. There they witnessed the difficulties of unemployment, especially for minority ethnic groups and women. One recalled: 'On my first workday I had a busload of Turks arrive off the plane, two weeks later a power strike and so we had an office full of State Electricity Commission workers . . . '. The other said:

> [It was] one of the biggest periods of unemployment in history. A lot of my clients were from minority groups. The Government had brought a lot of migrants in and there were no jobs. Also people from non-English-speaking backgrounds were higher in unemployment anyway. And there were a lot of Aboriginal people. So all that was very personally affecting . . . I remember having to explain to employers that were very, very racist what they could and couldn't ask for! That was my first experience . . . of the issues, the complexities and the narrow-minded attitudes of some employers . . . It was a real eye-opener.

The latter quotation is from the interviewee who had 'disgraced' herself by fleeing a claustrophobic set of parental expectations. The dislocation—physical and mental—that she had experienced personally meant that she identified with the transients with whom she was dealing in her daily employment. She also described a boss who profoundly mishandled people from different cultural groups, a negative example that remained with her in later corporate life. The whole experience 'made me hit rock bottom but made me stronger'. These experiences—the combination of reacting to oppressive family expectations, finding herself on the edge, engaging with others being treated unfairly—forged capabilities that equipped her well as a leader in workplaces containing a multiplicity of cultures, as well as reinforcing a powerful personal belief in 'the individual's right to be different in personality terms'.

Several of our leaders had first started work on the factory floor as young engineers, working alongside people of many different nationalities:

> I spent a lot of time on factory floors. I did a sandwich course—my degree was five years but it involved three sessions of six months in industry, on the factory floor—so I've been dealing with cultural diversity from day one, especially in my first ten years of work. There were multiple nationalities. I'm not sure if I'm any good at it but I'm comfortable working with different cultures.

This example illustrates the importance of those early career experiences in border-crossing. By the time they become leaders, most individuals are heavily insulated from the challenging, sometimes uncomfortable demands of directly negotiating with diverse constituents. But these early experiences 'in the firing line' continue to underscore these leaders' values and the managerial approaches they later adopt.

For those with apparently more predictable careers—largely remaining within the same firm—varied experiences in and out of working hours provided exposure, and insight, into differences. Many had started out in jobs where they mixed closely with people of different nationalities and educational backgrounds. One had driven a blind neighbour to his place of work for a couple of years, giving him a keen sense of, and empathy for, those with disability or disadvantage. This man's wife had re-trained later in life as a teacher of migrant English, subsequently moving into migrant education management and bringing the family more exposure to a range of different groups: 'That was another influence on me, developing friendships within different ethnic groups and invitations to functions which enriched you . . .'

One engineer had taken his first job with an overseas company in order to travel and be extended; his wife works with disabled children. Both these examples show how partners and children can provide an important additional influence in extending people's mental boundaries. Several of the men in our study mentioned that their wives' fields of work had indeed opened new vistas, bringing contact with people and problems that enriched and enlightened. Research (Sinclair 1998) has demonstrated that the experiences and voices of daughters, in particular, can be powerful influences in the decisions of leader fathers. Daughters can elicit a level of emotional attention and accountability from their fathers where armies of advisers may be ineffectual. For example, in the recent history of corporate Australia daughters have played a significant part in shaping corporate agendas regarding equal employment opportunity and environmental issues.

Variety in occupational settings has provided these leaders with a range of vantage points from which to view the world of work and of work relationships. Early professional experiences which place people in different departments within an organisation also help in this process of extending mental boundaries as well as extending specific skill ranges. So the engineer who does a stint in the marketing area or in human resources learns new ways of looking at people and problems. He or she learns that a marketing mindset, for example, is very different from an engineering mindset. It becomes easier to extrapolate to other diverse mindsets. Interviewees enthused about the enrichment they had gained, both personal and professional, from being obliged to work in other departments, even when the transitions had been difficult. Through the process of our research, one interviewee remarked on the connection between his advocacy of a change in organisational orientation and a resultant sense of identification with minority status:

> I am talking from a minority perspective in the sense that I have been a proponent of a more commercial, externally focused orientation, and this hasn't been an organisation like that. I haven't thought about it this way before—but I've probably had all the same kind of minority feelings that other sorts of minorities have around empowerment and disenfranchisement ...

There is no doubt that the experience of living and working overseas had enormous impact in a variety of ways on our subjects. The regional head of a major multinational company in

Australia recalled being sent home from his workplace in London because on a very hot day he and a fellow Antipodean had arrived at work in shorts and long socks. This was an early lesson in varying cultural norms, as well as an experience of 'outsiderness'. While providing him with a telling insight into the cultural specificity of what is deemed acceptable behaviour, it is also a good example of the differences that can be experienced in cultures that on the surface appear very similar. It illustrates the way in which small or superficial things can signal difference, erect boundaries and define insiders and outsiders.

Being in the racial minority was a powerful and lasting experience for a number of our interviewees. This was the experience of one of our leaders while working in Africa:

> I really got accepted into their culture and I also got a perspective on what it was like to be in a minority when I ended up playing professional soccer for one of their teams. I was the only white guy playing at that level so you go into stadiums with 40,000 people and it is the most frightening, humbling experience you'd ever go through . . .

One CEO described the benefit of overseas experience in early career in these terms:

> Going to other countries, learning the language, working with other people, is a fundamental—from my experience and also when I observe other people—is a fundamental experience to develop leaders who feel comfortable and pay a lot of attention in developing diversity.

An Australian-born CEO had worked in Taiwan:

> . . . where I was the minority. I was definitely clearly the minority and I knew how that felt. In my workplace too I was an Anglo-Saxon among 200 Chinese and the only one who didn't speak Chinese. It was very isolating and lonely, a very lonely experience. Work is normally a very social experience in many respects. But there you didn't have any social input to your life at work. That was when I really started to understand how it felt to be different. In the street some people would openly show hatred because you were white, and even spit . . . And I had to learn to change my approach . . . how you have assumptions that are wrong.

Outsiders

Turning to the border-crossing experience of outsiders, our own research findings and those of other researchers indicate that there are two phases—and accompanying organisational experiences—for people from cultural and racial backgrounds which differ from the dominant group. The first phase is from entry to middle management roles and the second is from middle management to leadership. Early career for those from different backgrounds is often a time of considerable mobility. It is sometimes also a time of organisational recognition and success. Many of our interviewees, for example, were on the receiving end of supportive rather than discriminatory experiences in their early career stages. The supportive factors included 'special' status; access to mentors; familiarity or comfort with shared colonial heritage; ability and/ or interest in sport.

'Outsider' interviewees, however, especially those from some Asian backgrounds, encounter subtle obstacles to their leadership aspirations as they approach upper middle and senior career levels. They are often tacitly disqualified from leadership roles because of their different style. A more consultative, indirect, group-oriented style is frequently judged as insufficiently 'tough', 'decisive' or assertive for a potential leader. They are more thoroughly tested and expected to get more experience, in more functions, than their counterparts from the dominant group. They are sometimes excluded from informal networks, so they have to seek out opportunities, not wait for them to come their way. Their careers are also more dependent on the intervention and advice of mentors.

The challenging influences therefore include high visibility, stereotyping and prejudice; extra tests of management and leadership potential; being locked into specialist or technical roles; discomfort with non 'command and control' style; and advancement by moving rather than waiting for promotion. Figure 1 summarises both the challenging and supportive influences at early and mid-senior career stages.

The evidence from other research about the pervasiveness of these forms of systemic and indirect discrimination is reviewed in Chapter 5. In this chapter our interviewees describe their experiences in their own words.

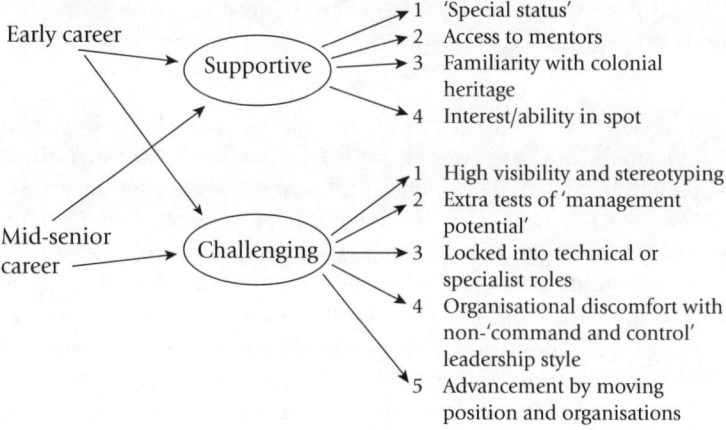

Figure 1   Career influences

Looking first at supportive factors, some of the outsiders leaders found their outsiderness lent them 'special' or exotic status. They had been marked out in ways which worked to their advantage. An interviewee of Indian background arrived in Australia while the White Australia policy was still in place. As the representative of a well-respected Indian company, he found himself 'effectively adopted' by a couple of local families. One woman later told him that he was the first 'non-white' she had met, 'and she was thirty-five or forty' at the time. Members of these families were pleased to engage with an articulate Indian on the issues of the day, and he was told that this contact influenced them to take more en-lightened political and public positions. His wife was 'one of the first sari-clad women ... and she became something of a celebrity herself' in many of the circles in which they moved. (Though, as we noted earlier, when she wore Western clothes she had been mistaken for an Aboriginal and shunned).

Often allied to this 'special' status was the significance for out-siders of mentor support in early and middle careers. Rather than sustained career support, in many cases the mentor's role was simply a good piece of advice or an introduction at a critical time. It is also worth adding that, by the time they offer this support, mentors have often had ample evidence that their mentees have special potential. Sir Arvi Parbo recalls how he got his first job with Western Mining Corporation:

> At nearly thirty years of age, I was much older than the normal graduate, and the Reader in Mining (at Adelaide University), John Morgan, advised me to look for a job in a small but enterprising mining company. He reasoned that a smaller company may grow faster, be less rigid in its treatment of new graduates and for both reasons offer quicker opportunities for advancement than the large industry leaders. He arranged for me to be interviewed by the Deputy Managing Director of WMC, Mr F. F. Espie [who was] based at Kalgoorlie . . . It was arranged that I would meet him when he stopped over in Adelaide on one of his visits.
>
> On the day, his plane from Perth was late, and he had another important meeting almost as soon as he arrived. John Morgan and I met him on the corner of North Terrace and King William Street and walked with him towards his next appointment. The interview went something like this: 'I understand you want to work for Western Mining', said Mr Espie. 'Yes', said I. 'Done!' said Mr Espie and that is how I came to join WMC. (Address to Old Scotch Collegians Association, 'Reminiscences of the Minerals Industry', July 1999.)

Most of the mentors cited by our interviewees were not immigrants themselves but were comfortable mentoring someone with whom they did not share a cultural background. These mentors seemed prepared to take a calculated risk, supporting someone different rather than someone just like themselves. In more than one case there was the suggestion that some aspect of the mentor's history, such as being an outsider or newcomer, prompted their identification with the more junior manager.

A high proportion of our sample of successful outsider leaders came from countries that had had a British colonial presence, such as India, Malaysia, Hong Kong. Being brought up in this environment meant that our leaders were familiar not only with the English language but also with Western legal and parliamentary systems and structures.

In addition, this background often led to a passionate enthusiasm for sports such as cricket. Sport was a potent uniting force among this sample of mostly male leaders. Our interviewees had frequently used their prowess in sport to earn respect and belong-

ing in the Australian community. Typically established in adolescence, sporting capability continues to be an important way of
bridging differences. Some had rejected sports associated with
their own ethnic background and determined instead to prove
'better than the Aussies' at their own game: hence the Italian who
rejects soccer in favour of rugby, the Chinese who became avid
swimmers or surfers. It is no accident that most of our successful
male outsider leaders were active participants in sporting groups of
one sort or another. But even without active participation, shared
enthusiasm for a game like cricket undoubtedly helps to break
down barriers.

There are, however, many challenges to be dealt with or overcome for those who come from somewhere different. Most of our
interviewees could cite at least one example of explicit or implicit
prejudice, based on their race or cultural difference. These were
sometimes experienced as a significant 'slap in the face', although
sometimes shrugged off with rueful humour. A mark of these
leaders might be their resilience in the face of such challenges.
Chapter 1 identified the following examples:

> I was sent to Melbourne and was talking to my manager to get time off
> to enrol in a Commerce degree. He said, 'Why do you want to do that?'
> I said, 'I want to get the degree and one day be General Manager'. He
> said, 'You'll never be General Manager. Number one you haven't gone
> to the right schools and number two you're not Anglo-Saxon'.

Another boss was explicitly racist: 'He said: "Only people from
cold countries make good managers". I told him that was rubbish.
I always spoke out.'

In their career paths, people from different backgrounds were
often not recognised as having 'managerial potential':

> I had a conversation with [my boss]; he was going to put me in a very
> senior position. I said he was totally wrong with what he was trying to
> do with the structure and he said to me, 'Do you want to be in the A
> team or the B team?' I said, 'I thought we were all one team'. That was
> the last I heard of that particular job.

This man had been put through the same management training
as an Anglo-Celtic colleague, but he found himself returned to a

technical position, while his colleague took on a senior management role. Eventually however, following a crisis and a turnover of leadership and board positions, his capability was recognised. He accepted the position of Australian Managing Director only on condition that 'I could do it my way'.

A number of interviewees reported experiences of effectively running a large operation but not being formally recognised as the boss: 'In a year my boss disappeared and I ran the operation. But they couldn't quite make the decision to give it to me. I was running it by default and it was going very well, but they weren't going to appoint me to the top job.'

Related to the preceding issue, these leaders often found they were appointed either to technical roles, such as Head of R & D, or specialist roles, such as Head of Asian strategy or Asia-area marketing. In this way companies could avoid confronting their own culture-centrism in assumptions of management potential, sometimes labelling different approaches as inadequate 'team skills'. Thus when 'outsiders' do well they are often marginalised under cover of technical proficiency. They are typecast as technical specialists and offered technical positions rather than positions which might lead to general management or CEO.

Differences in personal style can also be cast as a liability. In the following extract an interviewee reflects on how his own more consultative and adaptive style became viewed as weakness in an organisation accustomed to a 'command and control' style. Although this was one of many organisations that professed a strong 'team' orientation, the reality was much more autocratic:

> This migrant desire to fit in can be an impediment. I've had to, in some ways, downplay it as I moved into management—the sense of belonging to the team. Even though leadership today has changed more to coaching and influencing, those sorts of skills rather than command and control, there's still an element of that required, depending on the culture of the organisation, especially when you're relatively young as a leader. My natural inclination or desire from childhood was to lead by influence, but there are pressures on you to do more of the command, control stuff. So I needed to switch roles and decide which role was suited to the circumstances, had to be more conscious, step out of a natural inclination to be part of the team and say, 'Guys let's do this

together'. Now I sometimes have to say, 'Here's my view, please go and do it', which suddenly sets you apart. And for someone who's grown up wanting to be part of the team, because that's his childhood inclination, it is threatening to set yourself apart.

Another interviewee reports a similar discrepancy between the tough autocratic culture modelled by the CEO, and historically expected in the industry, and his own approach:

> My style and his style are completely different. He is like my grandfather where he truly is the patriarch. He's been very aggressive, truly gives managers a hard time. A lot of yelling and screaming—that's the way the empire has been built. My view is that's not the leadership style of the future—it worked up until this generation but not now . . . I'm sure I wouldn't have been a person that he would have picked in his own right. He would have seen me as too soft, not aggressive enough. When he's yelling and screaming, most people either defend their position or fight back. I say , 'I understand your position and I'll see what I can do'. That would infuriate him to start with, but he is a man of track record—he backs people.

It is perhaps not coincidental that this CEO who 'backs' track record is himself an immigrant and has a history of promoting people from diverse backgrounds into very senior roles. This aspect of leadership—the hiring and promotion strategies employed by leaders—will be discussed in more detail later.

Other research supports our finding that leaders from different backgrounds can't rely on waiting to be promoted in order to advance. By changing positions and organisations they accrue a track record of evidence which cannot be as readily underplayed or stereotyped as sometimes occurs within a single environment. It is as though these leaders from different backgrounds, who often also do things differently, have to provide more evidence of their capacities than do their locally born counterparts. Moving around can display a capacity to 'fit in' as well as provide a variety of referees with whom the 'outsider' can be checked. One of our interviewees said that 'in fourteen years I've held ten positions and always moved pretty quickly through the ranks'.

In a different sort of example, another interviewee had returned to work in her country of birth. Born in Korea, at the age of three she had moved with her family to Malaysia, where her secondary education later took place. Throughout childhood she travelled widely on holidays with her parents. She was then sent to Melbourne for tertiary studies. Some time after graduating, she decided to return to Korea to learn the culture and the language, obtaining work there teaching graduates wanting to take up further studies in the US:

> I had a very interesting time. It wasn't that easy. Being Korean by birth but not being able to read and write good Korean, speaking Korean with an accent. The reactions were not so good ... the students were very keen to get the maximum marks to get to the best US schools. They were very demanding, very serious about their studies. But it put me in good stead. Standing up now and doing a presentation is easy!

This woman had embraced the difficult option of returning to work in Korea even though there had been other possibilities at the time that would have been easier, less challenging. She now has a strong sense that she could successfully transplant herself anywhere. She had lived and worked in London and Thailand before settling in her current position as General Manager of a major division in a large multinational company in Australia.

Psychological pathways

Our exploration of insider and outsider experiences reveals the significant impact of border-crossing experiences which flow through into personal and work lives. These people have incorporated into their personal repertoires certain key orientations that have emerged from a combination of childhood and family experiences as well as early career experiences. These orientations can best be summarised as an openness to others, trust, flexible boundaries and a preparedness to challenge.

If we look into the psychological origins of these attributes it is clear that they are strongly interconnected. The large canvas of management and leadership is anticipated in our earliest experiences as we learn about the boundaries between self and other, about the nature of space and our capacity to use it creatively. A basic predisposition to trust or not, to be open or not, is often formed in these early experiences. We learn to deal with anxieties by either putting up strong boundaries or developing flexible boundaries: by holding on to firm categories and classifying what is 'inside' and what 'outside' or by developing habits of over-turning the categorisation process. We negotiate differences by retreating to what is known, or we may learn by experimenting, remaining open. We also develop confidence to be outside our-selves, to live in the ambiguity and vulnerability that this can entail, but then to develop robustness and strength from it.

We will argue that some understanding of these early inter-actions and experiences is essential to conceptualising leadership, and particularly a leadership that is adept at coping with change and difference. Of particular relevance are three concepts from the work of paediatrician and psychoanalyst Donald Winnicott. They are about space, trust and the capacity for cultural experience. Winnicott describes an intermediate area, what he calls a 'potential space' between the inner world of the individual and the external realities, between the subjective and the objective. It is in this space, says Winnicott, that children form their relationship with the outside world, first through attachment to 'transitional objects', such as teddies or bits of blanket, and then through play.

Winnicott maintains that two important dimensions of indi-vidual life develop from this 'space'. First there is creativity, meant broadly as a creative approach to life. Second, there develops the individual's capacity for cultural experience, a capacity located in the potential space between the individual and their environ-ment. This can develop only from a sense of confidence and, importantly, it requires trust. Winnicott says: 'There is a direct development from transitional phenomena to playing, and from playing to shared playing, and from this to cultural experiences'. Furthermore, he points out that 'Playing implies trust, and belongs to the potential space between (what was at first) baby and mother-figure', and that 'playing is inherently exciting and pre-carious' because it involves imaginative and emotional testing out and risk-taking (1971/91: 51). It involves constructing and nego-tiating variables that belong to inner psychological factors along-side dealing with external or shared realities.

Extrapolating from these important ideas, we suggest that connections can be made between the adult working experience of leadership and earlier experiences in the formation of identity that often leave lasting imprints. The connections between formative experiences and leadership are especially pertinent in a corporate world where some boundaries are virtual or collapsing and where local and global identities are being re-negotiated.

So we see that an openness to others and a genuine interest in others are core attributes for leaders who are good at operating in a multicultural, globalised world. Otherness or difference is not seen as a problem or source of threat, but often as an opportunity for personal growth, for intellectual challenge, for professional expansion. This openness rests on a fairly confident identity, a sense of identity not undermined when confronted by other ways of doing things. People who have this openness seem to have a balanced or moderate ego, robust enough to withstand and grow from challenge but not so inflated that the self can't step aside, appreciate and promote others.

This openness often goes along with both optimism and faith in others. Basically, people can be trusted. Trust is an important ingredient, but it is a trust that is tested by allowing and even enjoying the differences that others will bring. This is not the trust that says, 'I trust you to do this just as I would'. There is an important distinction to be made here between the trust that is offered to those who are 'just like me' and the trust that can be given to others who are understood to be very different from oneself. We are suggesting that what might lie behind this sort of leadership is not the clubbish trust of the team who all went to the same school or came up through the same organisation and share sporting and social activities. The trust required in today's leadership is more than being friendly or socially adept. It is based on enabling others to bring out their best.

Good leaders are flexible and adaptable around boundaries and borders, both personal and geographical. They can be comfortable on the inside, on the edge, and on the outside, at least for some periods of time. Rigid boundaries are not necessary for a sense of identity and comfort. Those people who practise this sort of leadership, we suggest, are able to belong but to be detached.

While they often have good 'people skills' and empathy, their sense of self is not defined by membership of a group. This finding connects to a distinction made by Zaleznik (1977) in early work distinguishing leaders from managers. Zaleznik argued that, based on their formative experiences, managers felt fundamentally more comfortable being part of a group—and were often lost without their group—while leaders were more solitary types.

Just as these leaders do not define themselves by, nor depend on, their own tribal identifications, they don't want other people to be judged by their racial, religious or gender characteristics. This sort of leader is different from the 'easy going' type who just wants to be everybody's friend. The successful leaders we have interviewed are interested in others, and keen to learn about others and about themselves from others. Their personal and intellectual boundaries are flexible. This flexibility has emerged from family dynamics and/or educational, migrational and early career experiences. Its continuation as a characteristic might have become more 'instinctive' than conscious, or it might be driven by intellectual challenge or by a more tacit desire for a different kind of engagement and relationship.

The varied ways in which leaders' experiences have been internalised and then found their expression in the workplace can be summarised as following a 'head' or a 'heart' path. Some of our interviewees had emerged with an intellectual view, often passionately held, that openness to difference (in people and methodologies) was essential both morally and for good business reasons. With this basically rational orientation, they sought out ways to enhance these 'open' attitudes and behaviours in their fields of operation. Others had a more instinctive feeling about this: a sense that there was simply no other way of operating. Theirs was a more emotionally based orientation, and we have dubbed it the 'heart' path. These leaders are motivated somewhat less by business argument, compelling though it may be, and more by notions of natural justice, equality and an automatic openness to other ways of being, thinking and doing.

This is not, however, an either/or scenario; people have moved from 'heart' to 'head' or vice versa at various stages in their lives and careers or in response to specific situations. They may also choose to put the case for openness and trust in 'head' or 'heart' terms, depending on which is likely to bring success. But their own basic orientation tends to remain predominantly intellectual or predominantly instinctive. There is no evidence to suggest that one or other modality is more effective, except in the sense that awareness of how others respond to the two alternative orientations may be helpful. This might affect the language, or tone, in which argument is couched and the circumstances in which to adopt a head or heart approach in dealing with others in an organisation.

As all of the foregoing characteristics imply, effective leadership requires a firm sense of identity, neither threatened by different ways of doing things nor feeling a constant need to prove oneself or retain an audience's approval. Backgrounds and experiences add the ability to forge on alone or even against the odds. Combined with strong values against injustice and faith in fairness, or simply a very practical mindset about the importance of capturing good contributions from people, this produces an enthusiasm for promoting the interests of others. In practical terms, these leaders are ready to challenge discrimination and to take risks on their own behalf and on behalf of others. This requires what has been described as a sort of moral courage that might set them apart, or elicit criticism or even attack from others.

The focus of this chapter has been on examining early career paths and pinpointing some core ingredients of a new breed of leader. We have argued the need to understand the developmental roots —personal and organisational—of leading well in a diverse world. This does not mean that capabilities and strategies cannot be learned and improved. Like the research on emotional intelligence, an understanding of the ways in which flexible leadership is developed will show us how to nourish and stimulate the necessary capabilities. In Chapter 4 we discuss in more depth these capabilities and strategies.

Capabilities and strategies: linking the personal to the organisational

Our exploration of leaders' backgrounds and early experiences revealed that they had been exposed to a variety of influences that we have summarised as 'border-crossing'. Those borders have included subtle emotional borders as well as the more obvious physical borders. Leaders with a background of border-crossing are potentially open to new people and new ideas and are willing to challenge the status quo in the ways they work in organisations. This chapter explores the organisational shape of border-crossing leadership, mapping the different qualities and emphases that are characteristic of this new approach.

To do this, we have drawn on and added to Kotter's framework for understanding leadership (1988). This framework is comprised of ingredients which translate into capabilities and are expressed in actions and strategies. Ingredients, capabilities and strategies make up three interlocking layers of leadership, from the underlying to the applied. While there are overlaps between these layers, which we describe, we believe it is important to show how leadership in organisations does not emerge from a vacuum but has its origins in the person and their history.

The ingredients of border-crossing leadership emerge from the crucibles of childhood, education and early career. Upbringings and early experiences elicit and encourage ingredients that include openness to others; capacity to trust; flexibility of boundaries (mental and physical); and a preparedness to challenge conventional thinking when necessary (Bartlett and Ghoshal 2002). These ingredients, we argue, are particularly suited to leading twenty-first century organisations—that is, organisations that are global in outlook and aspiration, that are transnational in structure and operations, and that are multicultural in terms of the demographic mix of employees and contractors. They require leadership that is not only comfortable with difference but can extract innovation and flexibility from this differentiation.

The ingredients put in place during childhood, adolescence and early career translate into particular capabilities. By capabilities we mean managerial and professional characteristics—dispositions and strengths—that are significant underpinnings to leadership in general but particularly to leadership which is adept in a culturally diverse world. The term 'capabilities' is used, rather than say 'competencies' or 'skills', to convey that these are enduring processes reflecting a combination of knowledge and learning as well as personality and emotional makeup (Dainty and Andersen 1996).

While these capabilities are a reflection of personality, they should not be regarded as immutably fixed at an early age or as unable to be developed. Part of our interest in separating out ingredients from capabilities is to make this distinction and to show how organisational and professional experiences can develop capabilities and enhance earlier acquired ingredients.

If one goal of this successful new leadership is defined as an openness to, or interest in, difference, our interviews showed that individual pathways to this goal varied. There is not one route but many in moving towards the capabilities and strategies we describe. Nevertheless, we discerned two main paths: the 'heart' and the 'head' paths. The 'heart' path tends to be driven by a more instinctive or 'gut-level' sense of decency, fairness and commitment to inclusion. A strong sense of identification or empathy with those who are different or disadvantaged by circumstance rather than ability often fuels this 'heart' path. In contrast, the 'head' path tends to be learned, is driven by logical argument and by experience. This path tends to the 'intellectual' view that drawing on the widest possible talent pool, unlimited by racial, cultural or gender characteristics, simply makes the best economic sense and will deliver the best organisational outcomes. The logic of this 'head' path is consistent with a tough-minded analysis of the human capital talent pool and a distaste for any barriers or obstacles that prevent the best people from contributing.

The fact that there are these two paths (and possibly more) means that the following list of capabilities is a guide to underlying characteristics which might take varying overt forms in the individual case. For example, all of our interviewees had an interest in others. Yet this took many forms, from a naturally friendly extroversion to a more courteous reserve. Importantly, it would be wrong to confuse simple extroversion or an abundance of 'people skills' with facility in leadership in a culturally diverse environment.

The capabilities and strategies identified here suggest a more subtle and complex combination of understandings about self and others, as well as a willingness to challenge conventional practice (see Figure 2). They also illustrate the general theme of this book, which is to posit a new, non-macho, anti-heroic model of successful leadership. These are not gung-ho, dramatic, swashbuckling attributes: they are subtle and low-key, and emerge more from a considered humility than a brash over-confidence. There is further evidence of the importance of humility—recognising one's own limitations and truly valuing the contributions of others—from Jim Collins' survey of leaders and the practice of what he calls Level 5 Leadership (2001). For Collins, the distinguishing mark of leaders who stand out is the presence of humility.

Ingredients of leadership

Reflectiveness

The importance of reflectiveness in leadership has been long recognised by scholars. In 1978 Argyris and Schon identified the capacity, indeed the habit, of critically reflecting on one's actions and comments, of assessing and taking responsibility for consequences, and of learning from this process about alternative future actions as a critical element in leadership. More recently, Daniel Goleman's work on emotional intelligence and maturity

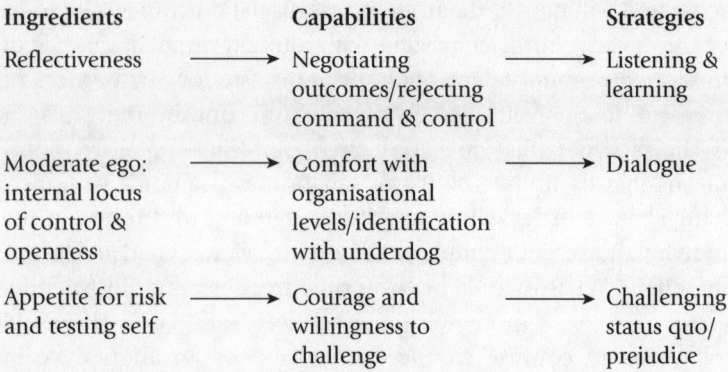

Ingredients	Capabilities	Strategies
Reflectiveness ———→	Negotiating outcomes/rejecting command & control ———→	Listening & learning
Moderate ego: internal locus of control & openness ———→	Comfort with organisational levels/identification with underdog ———→	Dialogue
Appetite for risk and testing self ———→	Courage and willingness to challenge ———→	Challenging status quo/ prejudice

Figure 2 Components of new leadership

has again pointed out the importance of reflectiveness. One aspect of reflective capacity is the willingness to be self-focused, to see how one's own history and style contribute to the way one operates and to issues and problems that arise. People who are unreflective are often very other-focused, and therefore tend to see the source of problems lying with everyone but themselves.

Most of the CEOs we interviewed visibly warmed to the opportunity our research provided to reflect on their experiences and to draw new insights about those experiences. In one sense, the fact that they were interested in the research and agreed to participate is a barometer of openness to reflection. But it became apparent that they relished the reflective opportunity of the interview itself. With very busy schedules, many had set aside the minimum time for the interview. Once engaged, however, it was often up to us to keep an eye on the clock and not overstay our welcome.

In particular, a number of interviewees volunteered that they appreciated the opportunity to talk about their own history, their families, growing up and early work experiences, because it enabled them to understand in more depth the roots of their current strengths—and weaknesses. One said: 'I haven't been this reflective for a long time. You don't get the chance to be reflective as much as you'd like. I don't in my lifestyle.' Some were initially guarded when asked about family background. However, they warmed to the themes, discovering insights and significant connections in their experiences that surprised them. For example, one connected the intensity of his belief in diversity with his own early childhood experiences:

> It probably comes back to the original questions you were asking me about who I am and my value sets. And my value sets of knowing what it's like being not included, having to fight for inclusion, that very definitely makes me try and always break that paradigm, on whatever account.

One test of reflectiveness is the capacity to recognise one's own biases and weaknesses—to be able to identify failures and discuss them openly. This was a CEO's discussion of his evolving views of diversity:

> My early thinking about diversity, which is not all that long ago [laughs] was a focus on very obvious differences. My whole thinking was how do you accommodate people who are different and make them feel part of the system . . . I think my thinking then was immature . . . it was almost like a patronising approach to people who had obvious differences and how could I be a good citizen and make them feel included . . . Being respectful and showing them kindness. But I now know that's a bunch of nonsense . . .

Moderate ego—internal locus of control and openness to others

The practice of this 'inclusive' new style of leadership requires elements which, on first glance, pull in opposite directions. We have characterised this ingredient as a moderate ego. The first element of a moderate ego is a robustness or confidence about one's own views. According to psychologists, a strong internal locus of control enables leaders to persist with their convictions without being overly dependent on the good opinion of others. Highly creative people often have a strong internal locus of control because they have to believe in an idea or product when others may be sceptical. In an organisational context, it is manifested in strong beliefs about what's right without the need to be popular.

The other element of a moderate ego is a genuine interest in others and an appetite for learning via relationships with others.

This sort of leadership is not threatened or frightened by 'other-ness' or 'foreignness' but asks, 'What can I learn from this?' A clear sense of self is neither too puffed up and inflated so that nothing new can penetrate, nor so open to the views of others that the self capitulates at the first sign of opposition.

An interviewee describes how ego prevented the MD of an acquired business from seeing how the business needed to change in order to operate outside its country of origin:

> . . . he has a very strong view about how the business should be run. It doesn't work at all. He's only used to doing business in his own coun-try where the customer and the MD is looked at differently. He speaks English very well, is very intelligent, but it is an ego problem. He feels he can tell the local guys what is good for them. We end up having big clashes . . . he thinks more and more of the same will change people.

In contrast, moderate ego allows an openness to new exchanges as opposed to an intensely competitive response where people come to work having to prove that they can do more than others or having to get the better of others:

> I would think managers that are less tolerant of diversity in workplaces are the ones who are the more black and white, either so by-the-book or needing such firm guidelines all the time that they can't see outside of that box. The ones who innately have a more caring side also have the ability to learn how to do other things, naturally. Some people are so keen on performing or proving themselves that they do the whole job themselves—it's not the way to get the best performance. It takes longer but if you get the whole team on board everyone will come out a lot better. The manager who does that is a better manager of diversity.

Other recent research has placed emphasis on the benefits of 'non-technical' personal abilities. For example, in assessing leader-ship performance, Daniel Goleman (1998) has found that it is much more closely correlated with emotional intelligence than with either intellectual/cognitive ability or technical knowledge. Goleman isolates five important components of emotional intel-ligence: self-awareness, self-regulation, motivation, empathy and social skills. Extending this argument to organisations, Quy (1999) suggests that while emotional intelligence equips individuals to be receptive to change, emotional capability in organisations enables them to realise radical change. Emotion-attending behaviours promote three conditions for change: receptivity, mobilisation and learning.

Foreshadowing this recent interest in emotional intelligence, Howard Gardner's earlier educational research (1984) added 'personal intelligences' to the list of those intelligences with which we are more familiar, and which have been more traditionally valued and measured in IQ tests: the linguistic, logical, musical, mathematical, spatial and kinesthetic intelligences. Gardner defined the 'personal intelligences' as involving two aspects of human nature and having certain core capacities, including both intrapersonal and interpersonal skills and sensitivities. These core capacities are, firstly, access to one's own feeling life and, secondly, the ability to notice and make distinctions among other individuals.

Consistent with our argument that we need to look further back in individual histories to understand leadership strengths and weaknesses, psychologists maintain that the development of core capacities for trust and openness begins with mother–child attachment bonds and evolves in stages through childhood and adolescence as people deal with various individual and interpersonal crises. Thus leadership research, educational research and psychological research all support the argument that these ingredients of reflectiveness and openness are important—and that they are developed early.

Appetite for risk and testing self
Successful leadership in the radically transformed organisational landscape often requires individuals, and organisations, to do unconventional things, make controversial appointments, adopt unpopular practices and tackle issues that other organisations may avoid. Personal shortcomings may need to be confronted, risks taken, mistakes made and owned up to. But our research revealed that another feature of effective leadership is courage and a willingness to challenge accepted practice. Courage, coupled with the capacity to reflect and learn from mistakes, emerges as part and parcel of the adaptability many interviewees had carried

with them from childhood experiences. The outward manifestation of this courage is not necessarily bullish or adversarial but is as likely to be quiet tenacity, persistence and determination.

One senior manager had been involved in disseminating to employees a high-profile program concerning the rights of Aboriginal people. A small group of staff on the ground in some states held some serious concerns. When the manager expressed these staff concerns there was scepticism from colleagues on the senior team, so strongly did they believe in the program's merits:

> So personally I felt very trapped at the time but we did deal with it in terms of more staff training and support . . . and I made sure that people felt if they wanted to talk . . . we made it as open as we could. Once we got into the campaign these people realised it wasn't such a big issue as they thought, it was more a fear for them, and we had a lot of success with it . . .

This interviewee reflected that gaining the assistance of the leaders of the organisation had been vital in working with the employee resistance as well as in ameliorating her own sense of being an isolated voice.

The leaders we interviewed placed great personal value on learning, openness and maintaining interests beyond their business. Some had an enormous appetite for the new. Reviewing their careers, all had been willing to put themselves in different situations and to see what happened. From this basic predisposition, we saw a continuum of risk-taking styles—ranging from the fairly calculating, planned and careful adoption of new roles (often in overseas countries) to, at the other extreme, a constant desire to test oneself against new challenges. Said one: 'as soon as I get into a comfort zone, I find another cliff to jump off. That's me . . .' Those 'cliffs' might take the form of relatively minor forays into new or potentially uncomfortable areas of business or social situations, or it might be a major change of direction. Courage comes in many sizes and shapes:

> When I was at school I worked in the drop-in centre where we aligned ourselves with the dropouts of society. I'm on the World Vision Board now. I could spend my life working for them . . . It is very important for me . . . I feel a bit constrained now this has become a public company

and I'm actually turning it into a company that's probably shortly not going to be the style of company I want to run. But I've fixed it. I like that. I don't want infinite continuity . . . I want new starts . . .

In the next example we see courage in the necessity to reach out to others, to put others at ease, even when you are the one who is the outsider. An Asian-born leader recalls:

> My experience in London really taught me a lot, it was a chance to immerse myself in a totally different environment . . . alone, no friend. Like all very big cities it was in that sense very cold . . . It took me a while and I realised that wherever you are you've got to go out of your way to be friendly, you've got to take the first step . . . take the trouble to make a friendly gesture . . . if you wait for things to happen they probably won't happen. I remember going to pubs in England and again you had to be the first person to chat them up!

Leadership Capabilities

Negotiating outcomes/Rejection of command and control

A number of the overseas-born leaders we interviewed remarked on what they experienced as a command and control style of leadership prevalent at the top of Australian organisations. Despite much talk of team skills, in their view there was limited evidence of genuine teamwork in the practice of executive cultures. Several of these leaders felt they had not been promoted to more senior roles because they didn't exhibit the traditional level of tough aggression:

> I think my people-management skills and my communication ability (it sounds like I'm beating my drum here) were definitely at a higher level than my peer group . . . just the ability to manage relationships, towards achieving a goal. I'm a very active negotiator, not in a formal sense, but I'll try and negotiate outcomes just through conversation and get people to see my point of view and I think that helps in an organisation. And if I ask myself where does that come from, part of it's familial, a very strong focus on making people comfortable . . . that and the immigrant background accentuated this ability to blend in and fit in.

I am not naturally abrasive. In Indian society part of showing respect is to stand back. In business environments that is a tough thing to battle against. I know my style has been seen in some quarters as soft, the way I manage, especially when people come from the hard-driving school of business management—the 'bash down the door' approach. Whereas my view is why bash the door down, just try and see if it's open first. People may mark you down for not being aggressive enough. There needs to be a level of aggression, or at least task orientation in what you achieve, that's natural in business. How you get there comes down to personal style . . .

These leaders saw team building as part of building a sense of 'family' and also, in practice, a means of encouraging the diversity they thought important:

We have this egalitarian thing, superior teamwork, we can deliver more. I am a great ambassador for harmony but you have to work very hard at it. I try to introduce gender and cultural diversity . . . it fits in with my philosophy of life anyway, enriches our experiences. One department I deal with doesn't have diversity and it makes it harder, they don't have experiences with different groups and different kinds of people, so the reality is that we have to deal with people in different parts of the world, if we have more exposure in our little corner then we'll be able to deal with it. Same with gender . . . I have more women in my team, though I don't go out of my way to do it, I find it very useful, more affinity to learn how to handle gender diversity . . . I wouldn't go out of my way, not without taking into account the merit or skill level.

Comfort with all organization levels/Identification with the underdog

The histories of the leaders we interviewed meant they were as likely to identify with those at the bottom of the organisation as at the top. They were intolerant of the badges of status and often more comfortable moving at lower levels of the organisation:

I really enjoyed working with working-class people. Straightforward, no bullshit. I liked the physicality of the work. I enjoyed the skills I was learning. I loved having the skills of truck driving and forklift operation . . . I enjoyed being the rebel as well. Even in those days, I'd be at an old school reunion. 'What do you do?' 'Oh, I am a truck driver!' I enjoyed that.

Another CEO describes how listening to the concerns of the shopfloor, which had never been done before, delivered a complete change of organisational culture:

> My approach is to go there, spend a lot of time on the factory floor. I'm an engineer, I love factories! I can identify with what they do. We have some of lowest award paid staff in Victoria—its a regional country town, but we're the only major employer. You need to ask, 'What is the pain here? What is the anxiety? What do these workers want?' Discover the hot button—'If I can't work who's going to look after my family?' So I asked the super fund how we can look after our staff if they can't work. Can we insure the whole workforce? It's never been done before. Got their rate down to 1 per cent. Go back and tell them as part of enterprise bargaining negotiations we've now covered you ... just forget about tensions, it was all done. If you can identify with the pain, with the anxiety ... it might cost 1 per cent of salary but for them it's a huge psychological boost ... It repositioned the company's relationship with employees overnight. It became a caring, understanding employer rather than adversarial.

Courage and willingness to challenge

The leaders are not afraid to try something new themselves. This often translates into a desire to challenge others—both people and systems—and a confidence in one's ability to make things work:

> I am somebody who will always challenge what is there and try to change it, hopefully for the better ...

> My tolerance for an environment that says, 'Don't change anything round here, it's perfect' is absolutely zero!

In some cases the desire to change is paired with a dislike of hierarchy and the pointless perks of privilege that may have built up in organisations. Our leaders don't insulate themselves:

> When I became branch manager, 80 per cent of my staff were Australians. One day the receptionist was sick and we were short-handed so I took over her place. Shows the team the bosses aren't just sitting in their room all day. Show by action, helps a lot ...

One CEO describes two earlier employers, both with traditional managerial cultures, as evidenced by status rituals such as reverence for an overseas head office, chauffeurs, silver service lunches and gardeners to maintain the rose gardens. When he was recruited as local MD, among his earliest actions was pulling out hundreds of roses and selling them to a local nursery. He was labelled 'a philistine, uncultured, I sold the silverware'. But as he describes it:

> I was not brought in to preserve a British hangover culture. This is a new world out here. We are a company not a nursery! I know they're beautiful but I don't want to spend time and money pruning the roses ... I expanded our factories, made us a larger local content factory rather than an importer ... It was almost like a cheek ... I'm different ... I'm a bit counter-establishment. That's why I disliked [previous organisation], everything so polished and perfect, there was nowhere for my creativity to apply itself ... I don't copy.

Here a leader talks about taking his organisation outside its comfort zone of compliance with government-defined gender quotas, to demand that people really ask themselves what was going on:

> In the US programs you had your percentages in little pigeon holes. You had to hit those percentages within three or four years and so the game was to hit the percentages and not be fined. But the buy-in was not there. It was mandated from outside so all sorts of ridiculous hiring practices went on. It also built a negative reaction ... But let's assume we have 50 per cent gender balance in our graduate intake and you have put in a process of staff development courses. If it's not fifty-fifty taking those courses, or within a band fifty-five/forty-five, something is wrong. Go and revisit it. If your input at this developmental stage is outside that range ask yourself why. There have to be extremely good reasons. If you're interviewing people for a job and if they're not coming in broadly the proportion you'd expect, revisit it. Why?

Strategies

Listening and learning from others

The strategy of listening seems so obvious to the sort of leaders we are describing here as to be hardly worth spelling out. However, some important accompaniments to the process of listening deserve highlighting. A feature of this listening is that it often includes recognising personal bias, changing an expectation or stereotype—as well as putting oneself in a one-down position, or making oneself vulnerable in being open to learning. It is not merely a physical or mechanistic listening. It is active listening, and those who are good at it seem to have an ability to get into the skin of the other person, if only momentarily:

> People come in here with these huge problems for them, their conflicts with supervisors, with the system or policies. You've just got to find your way through these things. Sometimes when you sit and take time to talk to individuals you realise the capabilities they've got and how dismissive you can be because you don't know people or because you've got preconceived notions about their status or contribution.

In Chapter 1 we described the formative experiences in Taiwan of one of our Australian interviewees who went on to become MD of his organisation. He had been taken by surprise by his admiration for a Chinese boss, his own emerging interest in Confucian thinking and his realisation that it was inappropriate to impose an imported management style, a Western style he had presupposed was superior. He listened and he learned.

In another example, this time in Singapore, an interviewee had to overcome considerable resistance from the local management. As he describes it, this process involved him tuning into his own sense-making processes and being reflective about traditional corporate stereotypes:

> I was initially oblivious but after a while I showed respect for what they had achieved over the years, and then I started to use them as sources of knowledge, saying, 'Well, how do you think I should do this?' . . . I think I garnered respect for doing that because I genuinely saw that they did have a lot of knowledge . . . We like to think we are far more open, less hierarchical. We like to think we're more forward-thinking. But the real issues that matter to people are respect and respect for achievement.

Dialogue

A number of our interviewees volunteered the importance of highly developed skills in reading emotional cues and responding appropriately. Certainly, all in our sample exhibited great charm and tact in the way they interacted with us. As we have seen, these capabilities have emerged from family influences, including position in the family, as well as from their own experiences as newcomers or outsiders who have learned to be sensitive observers: 'My background taught me to be sensitive to other cultures, also to be patient and to take the first steps myself.'

One CEO identifies how the difficulties he experienced as a child shaped his later approach:

> I seem to naturally slip into heart-to-heart dialogue with people . . . I suspect the 'feeling world' was being massaged as a kid and I've carried it through . . . But I think when you've been hurt and it's a silent kind of hurt, where you just take the blows and swallow it and get on with it, you become sensitised to the way human beings can throw daggers into each other. Being on the receiving end of some punishment tuned me in somewhat. I was lucky the hurt only lasted maybe a year and a half before the affirmations and the friendships became much stronger than those who were dishing out the punishment. Being a good listener too in those coffee shop years with young people who've had terrible family backgrounds and being a friend to them. Or being in tune with a disabled person who really wants to work the big machine yet he's got a steel rod in his spine that makes it an occupational hazard to let him anywhere near it. Yet spending six months getting him there and making it happen so that he can become a man because he got the opportunity . . .

Challenging status quo/Prejudice

An Anglo-Celtic interviewee talks about the difficulty he had in challenging racism at a head office meeting when he was still relatively junior. He argues that organisational support has now made challenging discriminatory behaviour much easier, and his own position and maturity have reduced the personal costs in speaking out:

> The Americans would always complain that the Asians were ineffective. I remember guys saying, 'Why the hell do we bother bringing them all the way out here, spending all this money and they don't contribute at all?' or 'So and so sat up the back for a whole week and never opened his mouth'. I didn't challenge it at the time—it was my boss's boss and I would have been dismissed. But I do now. I speak up now: 'You're the idiot not this guy' . . . The message doesn't fall on deaf ears

any more. You know you always had the CEO's support to pull people up and say, 'The reason this is happening is you're not providing the right environment'.

From another interviewee came two examples of challenging traditional prejudices against women performing particular roles in his organisation. The first concerned a prevalent view:

'She's a woman so we'll never send her off-shore' [to work on a rig]: I had to intervene in that a lot. I'd say, 'She goes off-shore. That's it. No arguments.' It's the only way you could do it. They'd say, 'It won't work' and I'd say, 'You will make it work'. Amazingly, six months later they'd say, 'It does work'. In the other example we bypassed our own people and went straight to the shipping company. We said, 'We'd like you to help us train Jackie'. So they took her in engine rooms across the world a couple of times and eventually we'd broken the barrier.

Reflecting on the issue of cultural diversity in the workplace, a number of interviewees drew the distinction between understanding it at an intellectual level and making it work by doing it:

My personal awakening really came with working in Africa and understanding that the only way to get things done was to not just understand the culture I was doing business in but actually to incorporate it. I could get things done 'my way' but nowhere near as effective as when I sat down, listened, experienced, got to know. Understanding is an intellectual level, incorporating is a doing level . . .

Personal leadership actions are critical demonstrations to the rest of the organisation:

It's often small things that make a difference—I've got one very talented young woman who now works from home because she has a young baby. It was either that or we would lose her because she wanted to spend time with her child, which I totally understand. I had to talk to the other people in her group because it is very different for us. Even when she and I have meetings here the baby is with us—there's always three people in our meetings and toys on the floor! You have to talk to your group because other people think, 'Why can't I work from home?' and the answer is, 'Well if there's a rationale I have no problem with it'. Her job involves a lot of research so it works well, but you have to look at the nature of the role. Other managers say, 'How do you do that?' I say, 'First you trust. I have absolute total trust in her, I know she'll give me more than eight hours a day. If she does it at ten at night or six in the morning I don't give a damn, to me that's not the issue' . . . It also sends a message to the organisation . . .

This chapter has explored how personal experiences shape ingredients and capabilities for leadership and how these in turn translate into strategies in organisations. Experiences of border-crossing—geographic, cultural, economic, psychological and emotional borders—leave a distinctive legacy in how these leaders approach the task of leadership. The themes running through the ingredients, capabilities and strategies are openness and reflectiveness; a capacity to trust, listen and learn from others; an orientation away from command and control towards more negotiated leadership; and an appetite for challenge and the courage to contest the status quo to achieve better and less discriminatory outcomes.

Such leadership emphasises a very different cluster of characteristics and capabilities from those traditionally valued in corporations. Other research is also identifying the emergence of a different kind of leadership. The authors of *The New Global Leaders* profile three leaders who they argue exemplify in different ways an emerging global leadership. The leaders are Percy Barnevik (Asea-BrownBoveri), Richard Branson (Virgin) and David Simon (BP). Barnevik is quoted as admitting, 'I feel a little ill when I see this kind of macho thing among American executives, . . . the list of toughest executives . . . "From time to time you have to shoot someone in the courtyard." Who do you impress by that?' (Kets de Vries and Florent-Treacy, 1999: 105).

Each of these leaders exhibits charismatic and empowering leadership and all are agents of change. They demonstrate this in different contexts: Branson builds a global organisation, Barnevik integrates a dispersed and diverse group of companies, and Simon transforms an ailing organisation. The authors maintain that these leaders perceive salient environmental trends before others do and weave them into a vision. This requires managing cognitive complexity as well as a capacity to inspire and energise. Charismatic leaders exhibit a mix of traits that come together in a driven but sometimes mercurial combination. They are dissatisfied with the status quo, restless, needing action, entrepreneurial, impatient but able to make others feel special.

In contrast to many other writers on leadership Kets de Vries and Florent-Treacy recognise that personality and character are important in understanding leadership. For example, an addiction to personal power means some leaders are fundamentally unable to let go and trust others. They suggest that retaining versus sharing power 'is one of the issues that distinguish great leadership from dysfunctional leadership ... The dilemma of leadership is that leaders of large organizations must juggle both external forces and the powerful undertow of their own character and their employees ... underestimating the personal factor produces unbalanced analysis' (1999: xxiv–xxvi). In the three profiles in this book, the authors seek to flesh out the character behind the CEO. For example, Branson's story starts with his career 'as a teenage business prodigy' and the authors argue that the Virgin culture is a replication of the values of the family in which Branson was raised; 'his leadership style is more or less an extension of his personality' (8).

The ingredients and capabilities of good leadership in a diverse world are not so unexpected. Prior research has identified the importance to leadership of reflectiveness, integrity and courage, empathy or emotional intelligence, and a strong internal locus of control. For example, Kouzes and Posner's model of charismatic leadership (1987) defines the charismatic leader as one who challenges current understandings; inspires shared vision; empowers others to act; models the way; and encourages the heart.

Difficulties don't readily deter these leaders. What we learn from our sample of leaders is that their remarkable motivation to achieve is, in many ways, a reaction to some of the obstacles they have experienced in life. They have developed repertoires of skills and abilities that perhaps their colleagues, who have had an easier ride to career success, have not. And, despite their focus and their emphasis on hard work, these leaders remain aware of larger social and global horizons.

The new contribution our research makes is to show the centrality and on-going relevance of these experiences in developing capabilities which are particularly well suited to running globally attuned enterprises, small or large, in the twenty-first century. It has taken the personal 'border-crossing' data across another border—into organisational actions. It has demonstrated the importance of early background and early experiences in providing an instinctive template for some people. For others, life and work experiences have forged a more empirical pathway from which capabilities have emerged and strategies have developed. These pathways—whether heart-driven or head-driven—can be used as models for individual and organisational learning.

Ambivalence about difference: displaying or downplaying?

Despite all that we have said about the significance of antecedence, for many individuals the experience of coming from a different background is, superficially at least, unconnected to their current practice as leaders or managers. Some see their background as irrelevant to how they approach their tasks—it is a side of them that is about family or history, not about who they are now. A number seemed quite surprised when we, as interviewers, made the connection between their personal histories and experiences and, for example, the way they develop or execute global strategy.

It is not hard to see why individuals would 'forget' their experiences or omit them from their working selves and identities. Their first and most enduring impulse may be to follow existing models, learn how to 'pass' as a fully paid-up member of the dominant group.

Immigrants and others who are identified as different confront persistent and endemic pressures to 'fit in'. These pressures come both from inside themselves—they want to belong and be treated without regard to background—and from outside—from peers and colleagues, from organisations and employers who too often see arguments for difference as 'special pleading' or asking for special consideration.

In this chapter we draw on our research data to reveal the complex pressures to assimilate that leaders experience at a personal level. In particular, we focus on our overseas-born interviewees' ambivalence about identifying themselves as coming from an ethnic or immigrant background, their ambivalence about self-identifying as 'different'. In their ascendancy to leadership in organisations, there are pressures to remain silent about the value of different experience (see Figure 3).

Pressures to conform

To understand the full weight of pressures to conform to dominant and traditional modes of leadership, it is essential to tease

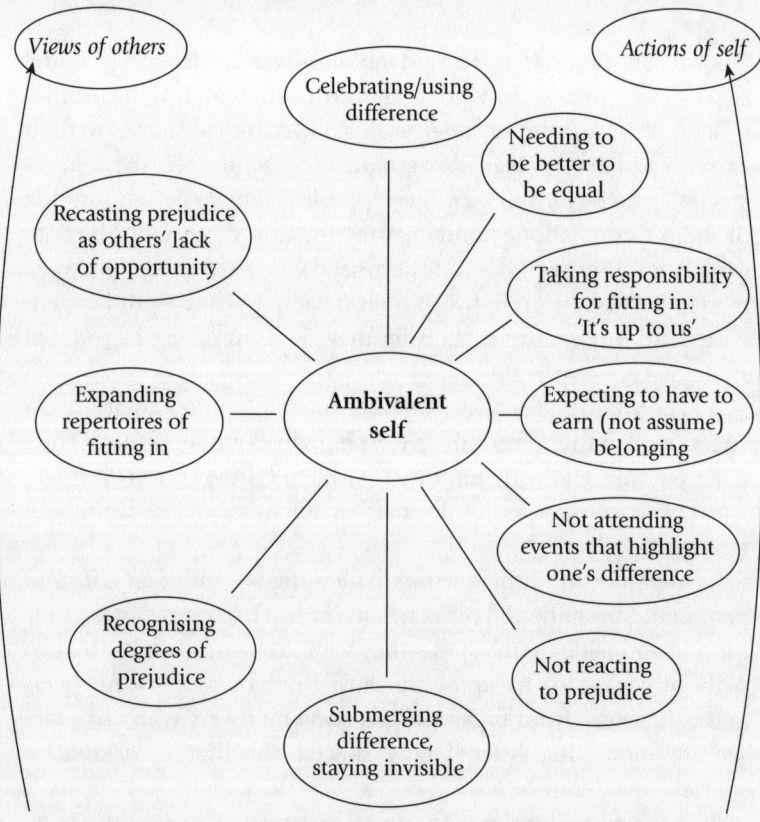

Figure 3 Ambivalence about difference

out the censoring and self-censoring of feelings and experiences of border-crossing and of being different. In fact there are enormous pressures on leaders to forget the legacy of their experiences and to assimilate to the dominant corporate culture.

In a newspaper interview, Jac Nasser, the Lebanese-born Australian former CEO of Ford, said that in his youth his way of coping with taunts about his difference was 'not to react':

> I was fairly desirous to be accepted, to not be an oddball that stuck out. If you reacted to insults and became an island of reaction, you see some people do that and it becomes a dreadful whirlpool of anger and rejection and hatred or whatever. That was never my paradigm. Bit of a humility process there. I don't react now. When mum and dad used to fight I'd just go to my room. I'd avoid conflict as a child. My chemistry isn't to be violent in response to abuse.

One of our leaders recalled similar strategies of not 'reacting' or 'overreacting', by which they mean not getting emotionally drawn into racially inspired insults or set-backs:

> Go out of our way to be of help . . . if there are unkind remarks I tell my staff, 'Eat humble pie!' I don't mean accepting bullying or unfair discrimination but don't overreact. That way you can win them over . . . I see it as a challenge . . . if I allow 'unfairness' to overwhelm me I'll not progress one step, I don't allow it to overwhelm me, from an early age . . . if I'm positive then my colleagues and my children will see it and be the same . . . I'm lucky in sense that I'm really broadminded, I don't see it as an obstacle, I prove it by my own action, my own deeds.

A number of our leaders describe actions which maximise this challenge: putting themselves in situations where they knew they would stand out, and expecting themselves to earn acceptance, one way or another. When one interviewee came to Melbourne to study, he chose a college where there were no other Asian students:

> It's a bit like a glass of water, I'm like a drop of dye—either I try to change the colour of the main volume of the water or the other way round, I assimilate and yet maintain some of my value set. Very much in the business world, because at the end of the day you're here to make profit for shareholders, you want someone who's prepared to achieve those sort of objectives and not to have a political or ideological crusade.

Pressures to 'fit in' were often so embedded that they were just part of childhood. With age and authority, some leaders now see that this intense pressure may have had some costs and that they now have more choice about how much they subjugate or highlight their difference:

> I was born in India but came here when I was five so bred here, but it's only been in recent years I think that I've really acknowledged the societal pressures, how that shaped my personality growing up. It's almost as if there's a common trait among immigrant children, a survival mechanism about fitting in, and if you're different in a predominantly Anglo-Saxon environment, which we were at the time, in Surrey Hills in Melbourne. There were very few immigrant kids there so we were out of the ordinary, you figure out how to fit in. As a family we had a highly attuned ability to fit in, almost chameleon-like into different environments. And that's good and bad ...

Such experiences in childhood made these leaders very tuned in to subtleties in discrimination. A number reported situations where others—for example Pacific islanders, Aboriginals or disabled people—had faced much more extreme (in their eyes) prejudice. This recognition of degrees of prejudice helped some interviewees overcome personal obstacles, and often gave them an interest in broader issues of racism and discrimination.

Another strategy employed was to recast discriminatory remarks or behaviour as aberrations or limitations in the perpetrator:

> You get drunken remarks sometimes, but I don't take that to be discrimination. I go out of my way to be helpful and friendly, and people most of the time reciprocate.

> I look at it from another point of view, not that they're discriminating but that they are conservative and narrow-minded, because they haven't had the opportunities, or the good fortune I've had, the exposure, the benefits of experiencing Eastern and Western culture. I know what it's like on the other side. You have to give them benefit of the doubt ... it's not that I'm arrogant about my culture, it's just the exposure one gets ...

Despite the determined stance of not condemning those who haven't had exposure to other cultures, non-Anglo leaders do

occasionally admit frustration with the narrowness of monocultural management approaches:

> Colleagues who do not share the same kind of outlook or belief or
> value system, I don't think one can change that overnight. The frus-
> tration is in . . . They are more narrow . . . they've maybe been manag-
> ing people or working in just one single culture, it's not their fault, they
> lack the exposure and experience which I've had the benefit of having
> grown up with and worked with . . . the challenge is we have to try and
> work together as a whole. Some people don't want to mix outside their
> group . . . I am a great ambassador for harmony, and it doesn't just
> happen, you've got to work for it, and work with others very hard to
> make sure there's a balance. Other departments . . . some very arrogant,
> they've only been to Bali or Hong Kong and haven't gone to the trouble
> of learning about other cultures . . . as a result you have a situation
> where you might hear remarks or unkind stories about me . . . They're
> very inward-looking, a bloc like all big offices . . . The challenge is to
> change that way of thinking. So leadership in this area is critical. I do
> things differently with my team. There's a lot of diversity . . . they look
> up to me and see the way that I do it, and it somehow shows in results.

However, differences do matter to others, and in the same breath
this leader goes on to say, 'Dad always said that because we were
strangers and migrants, whatever we did had to be better than, to
be equal to. We always set a higher bar than the people around us.'

Among our small sample, there were some differences in how
leaders interpreted having to be better to be equal. Particularly
among leaders from some of the Asian countries, being better
meant working incredibly hard, being very focused. And, these
leaders differentiated themselves by building highly cohesive
and effective teams. For some other leaders, commonly from the
Indian subcontinent, being 'better' depended on highly developed
interpersonal skills—being very good at making others feel comfortable—as well as being highly intelligent, all this often in a
modest and self-deprecating way.

Standing out physically can be a mixed blessing. Interviewees of
Indian and Asian origin continue to experience being the only
non-white face in many business groupings: 'It is still the same if
you go to any major senior business functions, 99 per cent of the

time I would be the only Asian in the room. Most Asian people don't feel comfortable so they don't go'.

People reacted in different ways to this experience. One interviewee reflected that colleagues sometimes envied what they imagined was a 'big advantage that you had because you were different'. He admits it didn't feel like that: 'I used to feel like hiding under the table because I was different. I used to be pretty cautious. I still am cautious'. Although he says he's now not worried about this, he does recognise that the expectation of monoculturalism affects others' reactions to him: 'It doesn't worry me but it does seem strange that I'm the only Asian there. People are very conscious of it when they first meet me'.

Another of our interviewees observed:

> Corporate leadership is substantially monocultural. Diversity comes from European Australians ... part of the European establishment. There is little or nothing to show for Asian immigration. People say this is a matter of time. We are only twenty-five years into our immigration policy, one and a half to two generations. People say that will change as our children grow up, have the old school tie and make it into the boardrooms [but] I attend events, committees, trade events and so much of our trade is with Asia, yet I am the only non-white in a room of forty or fifty.

Being different sometimes deters even the most senior of leaders from participating in what are often intensely monocultural business community events. Being successful clearly does not remove some aspects of being seen as a token. Among those who do participate there is also a sense of frustration that social and business events haven't caught up with the reality of who is involved. There is annoyance that the reaction of Anglo leaders is a focus on their race or their difference.

One interviewee elaborated the complex calculations he routinely still makes about how much of his difference he exposes, how much he is still learning about how to adapt. He also exhibits a strong sense of responsibility to work for change within these varied contexts—to move from being 'tolerated' to being 'accepted' and to ensure the next generation overcomes some of the obstacles. Asked if he was ever careful about how he presented himself, he said:

It depends on the crowd I'm in I suppose . . . For example, if I'm in a crowd where I feel they're all from Asia or Malaysia then somehow I will behave or say some things differently, without worrying about offending or that things might be taken out of context or differently. Then it's quite easy to fit in without having to worry. On the other hand if I'm with an Australian crowd I'm still learning a lot of things, I find that I become a bit more alert, I have to be careful in the sense that the last thing I want is to offend, even now I still do that . . . It is still a steep learning curve . . . You can't feel fully part of where you are until you're accepted. I don't want to be tolerated. I don't want my kids to be tolerated . . . it's a major difference. Being accepted needs a lot of hard work on both sides . . . the challenge is to be very proactive, to go out of the way, to be accepted . . . if the tangible manifestation of this acceptance is being invited to dinner at home with new friends so be it. I feel this is a challenge for my kids and I also feel we owe it to our future generations for everybody to do that because then our kids will have an easier time. We have a duty to pave the way for them to be accepted, in our social life, our personal life, as well as in our working life.

Another man had this to say about his decisions to display or disguise his difference:

You can pick circumstances, the radar is attuned to when it's of value to demonstrate the difference, and there are times when it's of value to play it down. For example, when I was younger and working in a sales environment, especially with tradespeople of traditional Aussie Anglo-Celtic heritage and background, you knew, a sixth sense would tell you this is not the time to play up the difference, this is the time to be as Aussie as Aussie! But it's something that's almost so natural to my way of being that it's hard to pinpoint. But today, it tends to be an ice-breaker—people ask where my name comes from. And then that leads into a conversation. I use it in the sense that yes I'm slightly different— I tend to celebrate it rather than hide it.

Under some circumstances leaders find they can use their difference to their advantage, eliciting the curiosity and interest that is stimulated by the exotic: 'Gee, who is this guy?' It can draw people's attention, which you can then use. An interviewee who recognised that his difference and multicultural experience enabled him to take a change-agent role reflected:

[I am] able to look at things in broad perspective, look beyond now and ask, 'Is there a better way of doing things?' Someone like myself can help be a catalyst, agent of change. Also I can ask a silly question— people don't mind explaining it to me because although I've been here a while it'll take a while to be fully accepted. But it helps to open things up ... the crack in the door, allowing people to listen to different dimensions. I can play the outsider when it suits—when new in a company, for example, but not for too long.

Asked about their own difference, a reaction among many interviewees was to ask, 'What difference?' They were surprised to find themselves given this labelling and some were testy about being included in this research partially on this basis. Nonetheless, they may sometimes 'discover' their difference in painful ways:

I had no sense of myself as different for most of my life and career. I was completely confident until I lost my job in a restructure. Until then my difference had always been a positive, a stand out. I have always been an individual.

Interviewees expressed multiple and sometimes contradictory views about difference. They also verbalised different views towards their own and others' difference. In relation to their own difference, there is a strong drive and desire to assimilate. There is also a desire, expressed above, not to have one's individuality eclipsed by group membership, not to be reduced, for example, to being 'Asian' or 'an Indian'.

Being labelled as different, or of a minority group, creates extra visibility, more stereotypes and more tests of belonging and performance. Difference brings with it expectations that one will be a spokesperson or advocate of 'ethnic' issues, with responsibilities to an identity group with whom one might feel reduced connection. On the other hand, interviewees shared a desire to have their history, knowledge and experience validated. They were angry and frustrated that sometimes their different appearance meant they were 'tested' more and excluded from eligibility for leadership roles.

Celebrating and drawing attention to one's difference is often the relatively luxurious position of those who are powerful enough or accepted enough to know that this won't count against them.

Under these circumstances some of our interviewees felt 'proud' of their difference and their heritage. For a couple, the readiness to act as an advocate for difference in ethnicity had increased with age, maturity and comfort in their organisational role.

Leadership that values difference

In general, overseas-born leaders are impatient with ideas about difference or diversity, which they often associate with heavy-handed government policy. There is an overwhelming desire to judge and be judged on the basis of merit. While this is rarely their own experience, it is the ideal they espouse. This senior manager sums up a common outlook:

> Diversity? My attitude is that it is potentially a strength and a weakness. I view issues of diversity—ethnic or gender or religious or whatever—very innocently. It's not in my psyche, so I'm not cautious. I do things because I regard my team, which is highly diverse, as all equals. So I don't consider it. I focus on the task, not on difference. I don't look at it as difference because I'm not aware of my own.

These non-Anglo-Celtic leaders have a vested interest in fairness, in ability and hard work mattering, not who you know or what you look like. For them, focusing on ability and merit has often produced more multicultural and mixed gender teams than is the industry norm. Many have impressive track records of building teams that are diverse because no implicit discriminatory barriers exist. In one case a manager won an affirmative action award for the high proportion of women in his unit, but he couldn't write a report on their affirmative action policies because he felt they didn't have any policies targeted to women. They simply hired the best people for the job, had developed a reputation for doing so and ended up with far more women than the industry norm.

Yet several of them acknowledge that it takes extra effort to hire someone different—not that the individual recruit needs extra assistance, but to ensure the organisation is open enough to let them perform at their potential. There is a particular sensitivity

aroused when hiring someone from the same cultural background
as the leader; it is possible that taking an active role can rebound
on both the leader and the new hire. The appointment can be
devalued as based on favouritism and not on merit:

> When I recruit someone, sometimes I find it even harder to recruit
> someone of different ethnic background because subconsciously the
> expectation has gone up a bit. So, for example, my Chief Financial
> Officer is an Asian Australian, from Hong Kong. But in order to take
> him in I went an extra step in order to make absolutely certain that cul-
> turally he can fit in. I do that to ensure that you have a greater success
> rate, because I know the requirements, the trouble it takes for someone
> to really blend in ... I know that these are some of the pitfalls that
> someone of that background needs to be aware of and I want to test
> that ... But the good news is that once you do that you can be quite
> certain and safe that the outcome will be good. I'm hoping that the
> reverse can apply too—that you would take the trouble or process in
> hiring anyone to truly understand the individual, regardless of race,
> how that person thinks, how he or she can fit in, or might not be able
> to fit into the corporate culture.

As noted earlier, many of our interviewees had benefited from
judicious mentoring in their own early careers. However, their
attitudes as leaders to mentoring or fostering those who share
minority backgrounds reveal complexities and some ambivalence:

> I would like to think yes, that I acknowledge the issues that have been
> part of my upbringing, of being an immigrant, so I suppose I empathise
> with people that are new to countries and have to assimilate and I
> respect the stress that that must create, the pressure to assimilate. You
> do it more by the people you deal with on a day to day basis. I like to
> think that I would think hard about how to assimilate people in a
> work environment, but I still think when it comes down to it though,
> business is business and what drives the bottom line, there's a lot of
> discussion about leadership style, spirituality and leadership, being a
> new way of thinking, but when it comes down to it all these concepts
> fade away if you're not delivering the bottom line. If one reason you're
> not delivering the bottom line is to do with cultural diversity then
> you've got a problem. Expediency might dictate that you take the path
> of least resistance and tend to only hire Anglo-Celts if that aligns right
> with your customer base ...

A number of leaders talked about the importance of developing an organisational culture able to accommodate and work with, not simply override, cultural and regional differences:

> In my first three months, a strike was building. I said to head office, 'Don't put in a performance—based system now, that will only put petrol on the fire. Let's defer it for twelve months. The view in head office was, 'No, we want to do it. Do it across the board, this year'. That was a disaster. You push as hard as you can with change but you've got to meld that change in with the local circumstances. That inflexibility at head office caused untold damage.

One describes a cross-functional team that is frustrating to deal with because it has no diversity. He points out the subtle and sometimes two-way nature of the problem:

> I can't pin it down, but we have to deal with them. It translates into a real loss for the organisation, and a real loss for me, because as a good migrant we want to contribute in more than just an economic sense . . . it's a challenge for me and down the track for my kids. That's why I get very upset when people hark back to 'in our country we do things this way or don't do it this way'. The problem can also come from the migrant themself who've come with the wrong attitude or not done their homework.. .it works both ways . . . we've got to be open-minded, be realistic, it's like any partnership, needs give and take, need to appreciate each other's way of doing things. Same in the workplace, we need to be working together . . . they must be willing to accept me too. My frustration is magnified because it is more subtle. I don't know how to handle it except to give myself more time. We need to work on it!

In our research as well as that of others in this field, leaders from minority backgrounds demonstrate mixed enthusiasm about identifying with and supporting their own communities in business. Asked if he acted as a spokesperson for his ethnic community, one leader said:

> No—I consider myself a representative of a minority within the business community but I can't speak for people in general as ethnic minority. I don't feel it as a burden but as a compliment that I can help to spearhead a bit the corporate sector into doing things with a more international or global dimension.

He attends some business forums but is not very active: 'I've enough alligators to capture in my own backyard!' Another leader argues:

> I've resisted being used as a—I've had a couple of [ethnic] community groups chase me to support a charity or meet a visiting dignitary or something. I haven't said 'No' but I've just tried not to . . . I'm busy. It just falls off the tree in terms of priority. My high priority is doing what I need to do and if it happens to be slightly skewed to diversity then that's fine but it's not a spokesman advocate-type role.

In a couple of cases these leaders are active in ethnic chambers of commerce or business associations, but they make calculations which suggest that such participation can sometimes reduce their credibility and capacity to talk on generic business issues. Once a leader is identified as an 'ethnic' business leader, this can sometimes reduce or marginalise their broader business contribution.

Does the possession of formal power liberate leaders to be more outspoken about the values of different experiences and perspectives? Taking on the role of CEO, MD or Chairman should, in a sense, free leaders to be more open and expansive in their views on diversity. Yet for reasons we discuss in the next chapter this does not seem to happen, with leaders often feeling more pressured to censor and qualify their views when in a formal position of leadership.

For most Australian organisations, diversity is simply not on their agenda unless they are reacting to particular issues. Reactive reasons include highly publicised failures in managing diversity: for example, a senior woman launching a lawsuit for discrimination, or widely publicised and expensive failures in overseas operations. As many high-profile cases have shown, Australian companies have often expanded into new overseas markets insufficiently knowledgeable about and prepared for the cultural and other differences they will encounter. Although this is often starkly the case for companies moving into the Asian region it can also happen in Europe and the United States, where cultural commonalities are assumed.

But there is, increasingly, an appetite to understand Asian cultures as a means of leveraging global expansion plans. Selling this message about diversity now encounters much more receptive audiences. One of our interviewees of Chinese background had an extended period working in Asia. In five years he set up eight new operations in Asia, working one week in Australia and one week in Asia. This was followed by another three years when he and his family lived in Kuala Lumpur, where he built two more plants and ran several businesses. Returning to Australia he didn't see eye to eye with the Australian MD and instead spent time 'on the talk circuit' speaking on 'how to set up businesses in Asia'. In his audience at one of these talks was his current employer, who highly valued his experience of working across diverse Asian cultures and didn't simply pigeon-hole him as a start-up manager for Asian operations only.

But the other parts of the diversity message generate much less interest among corporate leaders. This interviewee describes how his corporate CEO colleagues have responded to his business interests since he has become non-executive Chairman:

> There are two main areas of my interest—one is IT and the other is multiculturalism. Now that I am non-Executive Chairman, I make myself available to give talks ... I have had the experience of saying, 'Well, what I'd like to talk about is the benefits of diversity, how to manage a diverse workforce'. People will come back and say, 'That's really nice, that's fantastic, interesting, but we've done a bit of a ring around and what they really want you to talk about is electronic commerce. It is quite frustrating, almost humiliating. I like to feel I have achieved something in this area, I'm proud of what has been achieved. To offer and then get 'thanks, no thanks' ... Now how I handle it is this: if it's IT-related I'll do it for a fee, if it's diversity-related, I'll do it for nothing.

Among other leaders there is a strong conviction about not letting any differences stand in the way of people working hard and being rewarded fairly. This faith in the capacity of business to bridge difference is reflected in the remedies for Australian awkwardness in Asia. It also translates into an antipathy to government-mandated diversity and a desire to distance from what are perceived as non-core issues:

Business has become more hands off [towards social issues]. It's probably part of the trend towards economic rationalism, fundamentalism. Very much this thing you must focus, you must maximise share price, profit. People are overworked. They have to make choices.

Thus, opportunities to advocate diversity issues often reduce with increasing authority, particularly if leaders are seen to be proactively discriminating in favour of diversity. Increasing formal authority brings with it greater visibility, as well as the envy of peers or subordinates who are looking for evidence of weakness to attack. An interviewee recounts his experiences in IBM and compares it with his efforts in an Australian subsidiary:

At IBM I could stand up and say 'I'm Indian, we need recruits, we should try India as a source'. It was a very mature culture. This environment is more street-fighter, passionate, bitter. We were desperate for people. I went to a well-respected Indian firm and got them to send four guys. They were seen as 'my people'. There was a very bitter dispute, partially to do with sales force versus other internal cultures. The whole floor moved and didn't tell these guys. Two were left on a whole floor on their own. I felt terrible about that.

Pressures to assimilate and experiences of bi-culturalism

The institutional barriers to people with minority backgrounds assuming management and leadership roles are complex and subtle. Anti-discrimination legislation has addressed, and reduced, discriminatory barriers to entry at recruitment levels of the organisation. At graduate entry level and junior management, organisations are increasingly diverse as they reflect the diversity of their pools of educated graduates. So while 'getting in' has become less of a hurdle, 'getting up' into senior and leadership ranks remains a path littered with unconscious and tacit barriers for those judged as different.

In much of the early managerial literature the obstacles faced by people perceived as 'different' were treated as individual deficiencies among members of that group—a lack of education, training or experience in line management roles (see Sinclair 1998 for a discussion of this 'pipeline' argument). Not infrequently, managers and leaders have argued that these obstacles will disappear with time, as people from minority backgrounds gain appropriate training and experience to assume leadership roles. While there is some evidence that stereotypes and prejudice do break down as people from different backgrounds get increasing opportunities to work together, the statistics indicate that pervasive systemic obstacles remain.

More recent research has shown that barriers are more likely to lie in how people who are perceived to be different are judged and reacted to by members of the dominant group, as well as how these judgements are reflected in institutionalised systems in organisations. These barriers include stereotyping and prejudice; tokenism and high visibility; being expected to act as a representative and advocate for one's group in addition to normal duties; an absence of role models, sponsors and mentors; and indirect discrimination mechanisms, such as exclusion from informal networks and social rituals, being subject to extra tests of managerial ability, and being paid less for the same work

In their American research, Thomas and Gabarro (1999) cite the Glass Ceiling Commission, which has shown that the number of minority executives in American organisations is at a very low level and has barely doubled to just over 2 per cent in the decade 1982–1992, despite anti-discrimination measures. Thomas and Gabarro conducted twenty case studies of minority executives in three companies, and thirty-four comparisons of white managers and minority managers. They found that the career paths to senior executive positions were different, with minority managers experiencing a 'tax' or lag. Recognition of these managers' talents came more slowly, was subject to more 'tests' or was simply not assumed as in the case of whites. The career path for white managers through early, middle and senior levels was characterised as fast, fast, slow. For minorities it was a 'punctuated equilibrium' with slow to moderate progress to middle management. Thomas and Gabarro conclude that 'different sets of rules govern white and minority attainment. Fast early promotion rates significantly increase the likelihood of a white reaching the executive level, while no such relationship held for minorities' (1999: 71). They offer three reasons for the career path differences: prejudice; white managers' needs for comfort and avoidance of risk; and institutional obstacles to identifying minorities as being of high potential.

Derek Dingle's profiles of eleven black American CEOs feature those who have started out as entrepreneurs, breaking into white-dominated industries and building large and successful enterprises. Their histories showed that most have endured significant, race-related hurdles including poverty, being denied basic opportunities (such as bars on black recruitment), or denial of a bank loan on the basis of race. A number grew up under regimes of segregation, going to black-only schools and travelling on segregated public transport. Others were the children or grandchildren of slaves. Dingle summarises the three main hurdles faced by this group as 'lack of capital, diminished access, and outright racism' (1999: xi).

The hardships and struggles of black entrepreneurs and their families have left legacies including remarkable determination and a desire to succeed. In some cases there is also a strong commitment to their communities—for example in recruiting and developing black employees and supporting community initiatives, such as the Essence Annual Black Music Festival. The founder of Essence Communications Inc, Clarence Smith, launched this event in 1995 as part of their corporate philosophy, 'Do Well by Doing Good'. Their commitment was tested shortly after in 1996 when Louisiana's state legislature, along with a number of other American states, was considering new legislation banning affirmative action initiatives. Smith and his colleagues successfully lobbied the state to remove the legislation from consideration, and subsequent music festivals went ahead. Another CEO in this group, Byron Lewis, has his identification with his community enshrined in his corporate mission: 'to become the nation's largest multicultural advertising agency' (Dingle 1999: 94).

In the stories of these CEO's success, as well as their own personal qualities, external sources of support have been important. Mentors, both black and white, figure prominently. Some institutional initiatives have provided explicit opportunities for blacks. One found his abilities nurtured in the Army: 'It was really the first level of corporate training that blacks received ... You were able to manage men and money as well as provide leadership. When the affirmative action days came, army officers were among the first [black] people that I saw going into corporate America' (Dingle 1999: 97). Another CEO benefited from the training provided by Ford as part of its Black Dealers Training Program.

Researching the experiences of black professional women, Toni Denton (1990) shows that these women experience extra pressures in their organisations which translate into extra needs for sponsorship and support. At the same time, black women are often excluded from two of the traditional mentoring/support structures in organisations: the master–apprentice system of grooming leaders, and the old or new boy informal rituals centred around drinking, sport and socialising.

In a study of thirty women managers, interviewees described 'having to cope with the double negatives associated with both racism and sexism'. Interestingly, most regarded their colour as 'a greater barrier' than their gender (Davidson 1995: 27): 'In addition, many of the major problems were linked to their role as the token black woman, such as performance pressure, racial stereotyping, isolation and lack of black role models, visibility, tokenism and "ghettoisation" (being directed into narrow areas of specialisation reserved for token groups), and being a test case for future black women managers'. This is a sample of their comments:

> People see black—they don't look at your contribution.
>
> Being an Asian woman, I'm expected to be submissive, but in reality I'm totally the opposite.
>
> Being a black woman and consequently being discounted ... always having to prove that you're not a fluke.

There is little research specifically on the experience of black—indigenous or immigrant—managerial women in the Australian context, or work that focuses on the experiences of managerial women from Asian and Indian backgrounds in Australian organisations. However, research on women migrants to Australia has shown how highly skilled migrant women seeking to access professional and managerial positions face double discriminatory loads. These professional women thus face particular barriers at recruitment—those described by Ian Watson (1996) as 'the glass door'—which are worsened by the interaction of gender effects. Women have to unlearn patterns of behaviour appropriate to women in their home country and to learn new patterns of self-presentation: to market oneself, to engage in confident eye contact, to list and describe one's achievements.

In Blackwell's study (1981) of the effects of policies designed to assimilate or 'mainstream' black professionals into white institutions and communities, blacks adopted one of two behavioural responses: assimilation or compartmentalisation. Assimilation involves conforming to the values and norms of white society, whereas compartmentalisation requires shuttling between two cultural contexts, each with their own norms, expectations and loyalties.

Bell (1990) explores a third option she refers to as biculturalism. The 'bicultural life experience' of the black woman manager requires that she 'create a dynamic fluid life structure that shapes the patterns of her social interactions, relationships and mobility, both within and between the two cultural contexts' (462). Biculturalism has both advantages and costs. It permits a black woman to 'hold on to her Afro-American rootedness without being totally assimilated into the dominant white culture and it permits her to enter the predominantly white world' (462–3). However, it also condemns the bicultural person to marginality—to not being wholly accepted by either culture.

Being bicultural provides richness, strength and resources to an individual's life, but it also introduces pressures to suppress one or other cultural identity, and imposes extra work in meeting expectations from both sides. Individuals living a bicultural identity feel themselves to be two people or living two different lives, with access to quite different sources of power, status and identity operative in each. Problems arise when operating consistent with one context jeopardises the necessary support and efficacy in the other. In other literature this tension has been described as occupying a 'divided consciousness', which involves 'clicking in and out' between identities. A study of black policeman in America teased out some of the difficulties—white colleagues waiting for black police to show favouritism to blacks, and black offenders taunting black police for upholding white law (Alex 1969). A response of black police that has been documented in other research is to be tougher on offenders of their own race, rationalising that this disadvantages the offender less than would accusations of favouritism.

This American research literature highlights the fact that social identity conflicts can be a routine part of the organisational experience of minority managers. Those managers deal with this largely by adopting individual strategies which have been learned through experience. Drawing on two studies of black managers in the early 1990s, Elmes and Connelly describe the constraints on this repertoire:

> ... black managers spoke of the everyday putdowns and humiliations they experienced but could not discuss for fear their white colleagues would interpret them as exaggerations, as unsubstantiated claims of racism. From this perspective 'diversity' is embraced as long as members of lower status groups avoid bringing up issues and themes that are too far removed from the shared experiences of the majority in the organization or that might reflect poorly on members of the dominant group (1997: 158).

Power and one's position in the organisation are important determinants of whether and how one can raise race or ethnicity issues. However, for the reasons discussed earlier and even when they are the boss, not all leaders from minority backgrounds choose to champion these issues in their organisation or in public forums.

This chapter has explored the ways in which Australian leaders from many cultural backgrounds and with a diversity of experiences manage and incorporate differences in their approaches to leadership. Despite an array of ways of ignoring and dismissing their own differences, leaders do feel different in many circumstances. There is no doubt that in their experience, unfairness and discrimination happen. This is a source of frustration, disappointment and occasional humiliation if they allow themselves to dwell on it—which is not very often. They are matter-of-fact that they are perceived as different in the Australian marketplace and that this can constrain what they do. One Asian CEO of an Australian company, in response to a question about situations in which he felt different, said 'I'm always different'. Similarly, another Asian MD of a traditionally very Australian business prag-matically excludes himself as the public face of the business, saying, 'I'm a realist'. An Indian admitted, 'I can't conceal therefore I accept it. I focus on the task'.

We were intrigued by how, over the course of one interview, our participants could move between denying their difference, ignor-ing their difference and being highly conscious of their difference. In their own approach to their careers they often argue they have had to be much better, because of their difference, to be equal or to have something close to equal opportunities. Towards others they typically maintain a position of being resolutely uninterested in any differences other than ability and potential. There was a mixture of responses to what were perceived as government-directed attempts to highlight or orchestrate difference to some social policy agenda, ranging from irritation to regret that such intervention might be necessary. There was also impatience with those who used their difference as an excuse for non-achievement of tasks or goals. At the same time there was a recognition that in their approach to managing and leading, they often adopted radically different values and strategies from those traditionally adopted in their organisations.

To make sense of these various positions we draw on post-modern and poststructural perspectives which do not seek a single unitary and fixed interpretation of 'what's going on'. In simple terms, individuals may adopt multiple sense-making perspectives on their identity and their role in their organisation. Each has legitimacy and value for different contexts: understanding one's own history, leading others, working alongside other business leaders, setting personal goals and objectives. Poststructural theory recognises that individuals will frequently adopt appar-ently contradictory positions; rather than compromising their position, this is an adaptive process that enables them to operate in multiple ambiguous contexts.

While recognising that systemic disadvantages accruing to non-whites in Australia might be a useful understanding in one context, it might be undermining to action or debilitating in another. In this way, having multiple ways of making sense of experiences of discrimination is not a liability but an essential part of the tools of diversity leadership. Being able to selectively ignore, screen out or celebrate one's difference has been functional to the continuing success of the overseas-born leaders in our sample.

Further, postmodern work shows that identity is not a fixed single construction which the individual determines in advance then lives out. Rather, the self is formed and re-formed according to the opportunities and constraints presented by different contexts and audiences.

The performances that are part of identity formation are 'a continuous process of narration where both the narrator and the audience formulate, edit, applaud and refuse various elements of the constantly-produced narrative' (Czarniawska-Joerges 1996: 160). We capture this fluidity in identity construction around difference in Figure 3 (p. 76). Views of others and actions of self are modified and adopted according to the context—from 'fitting in', through ignoring prejudice and recasting discrimination to celebrating one's difference as a source of value and contribution. Leaders move around this territory of ambivalence without too much apparent strain or conflict. Rather, they develop highly sensitive ways of judging how much to play down or how much to display their difference.

The context for leadership

The idea of leadership as the property of outstanding individuals, without regard to their cultural, economic or political context, remains appealing. However, in this chapter we argue that to understand traditional leadership, and to appreciate the obstacles to new forms of leadership emerging, we need to pay attention to how history and business ideology shape expectations of leaders and limit opportunities for new forms of leadership (see Figure 4). Our focus here is on the structural conditions for leadership— the circumstances embedded in economic conditions, cultural myths and business ideology.

Business and management thinking has given us one view about what leadership should look like: a heroic, individualised performance that privileges toughness, self-reliance and emotional stoicism. We analyse first how this leadership ideal narrows opportunities for other ways of leading to emerge. A second set of challenges for leaders who work with difference includes economic conditions and prevalent business ideologies that set expectations for leaders and managers. In a business environment of lean organisations, doing more with fewer resources, business time horizons become shortened and managers are often operating in survival mode. These conditions reduce opportunities for experimentation and for learning, as people rely on what has worked in the past rather than trying something different. The

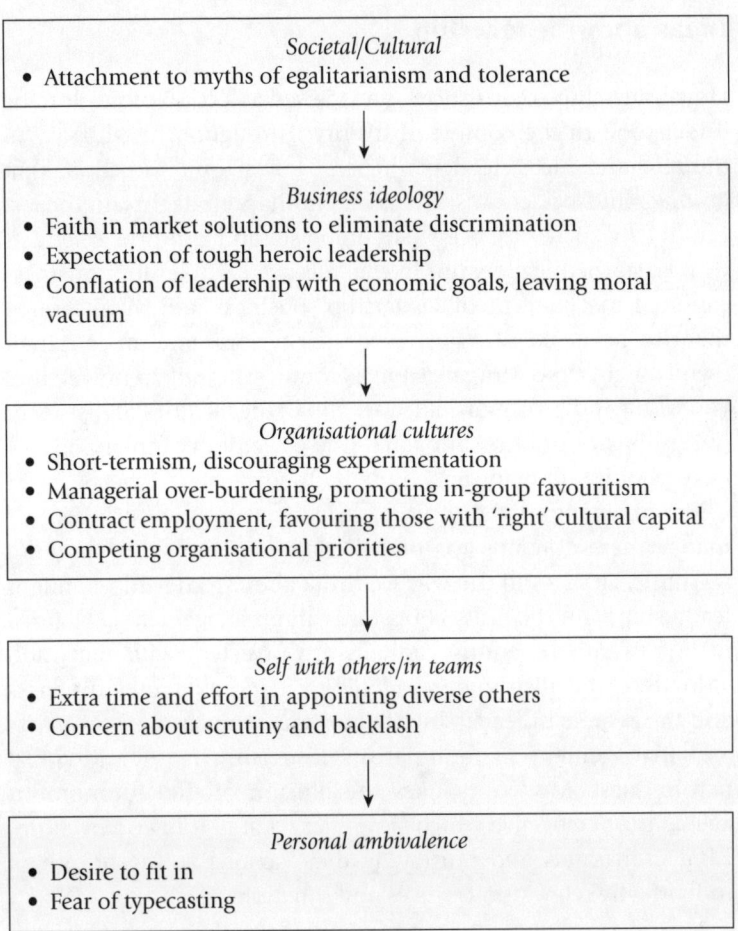

Figure 4 Pressures on leaders not to advocate difference

third set of issues that provides a limiting context for leadership arises from entrenched attachments to the ideal of Australia as an egalitarian, non-racist society. In business environments there remains a widely held view that the best form of mateship will ensure that merit prevails.

Ideas about leadership

How leadership is constructed and viewed as a concept needs to be understood in the context of history. Throughout the history of thought and ideas, leadership has been a topic of scholarship among philosophers, historians and military strategists. In the last century or so it has been psychologists and political scientists who've studied leadership. In the late twentieth century business captured the concept of leadership. Business and management theorists have taken leadership to their bosoms and made it their own (Knights and Morgan 1992). Now, if you look at universities you won't find professors of leadership in the faculties of history or philosophy or politics, but you'll find a plethora of them in business schools and management departments.

The annexing of the topic of leadership by the business and management domains accomplishes a number of subtle, and not so subtle, changes in the way we think about leadership. It aligns leadership with the tasks of business and management as defined in late twentieth century capitalism. Consistent with that individualistic and instrumental ideology, it individualises the tasks and the bearers of leadership. For example, much of the business and management literature treats leadership as an individual heroic quest. Modernity likes the illusion of the 'autonomous agent': the perspective which simplifies what is going on by atomising individuals and portraying their actions as the output of individually relevant incentives and sanctions.

This is convenient and appealing for several reasons. Our contemporary view of leaders as stand-out individuals without contexts or backgrounds should be understood as part of a broader culture which lionises individual achievement and is dismissive of the collective. It says a great deal about the intensely individualistic ideology of late capitalism, but renders undiscussable and illegitimate many important aspects of leadership behaviour: dark sides and neuroses, physicalities, sexualities and bodies.

If you want to seek explanatory closure, this idea of leadership is also useful: CEOs either have it or they don't; and if they turn out not to have it, you can sack them. It thus allows everybody else to abrogate their responsibilities for thinking about what they didn't do. The problem is simply diagnosed, and dismissed as 'lack of leadership'.

Another reason why leadership as individual performance is attractive is that it allows a focus on heroic deeds, on spectacular feats of endurance, great tales of triumph over odds and extraordinary self-sacrifice. As was argued in *Trials at the Top* (Sinclair 1994), we are a society in which men, in particular, are starved of opportunities to see themselves and their contribution in a wider sense. Great corporate acts of leadership are the contemporary equivalent of the journey of Ulysses: fighting off the sirens, resisting temptations and weakness, finding a way between the twin horrors of Scylla and Charybdis. Great corporate deeds, or the prospect of them, feed a mythic hunger that is not well nourished in a society as secular as ours.

Within the business literature, leadership is often recast as warfare: the task is doing battle with predatory competitors, scheming regulators and recalcitrant employees. Phrases like 'winning the war for talent' may be metaphors but they also transform the experience. The metaphor becomes reality as the language-in-use of training programs and performance management schemes.

The business community has a vested interest in advancing its own members as exemplars of leadership. Events like the World Economic Forum encourage us to collapse the categories of world leader and corporate chief. When people think of leaders they are increasingly likely to think corporate leaders. Business also has an interest in arguing that the corporate environment provides one of the best testing and breeding grounds for leadership qualities.

The blurring of these categories treats the achievements of corporate leadership as the achievements of leadership. Qualities such as singularity of purpose and determination to advance company goals and increase the share price come to be elevated, while other qualities such as compassion, empathy or breadth of life experience get deleted from the leadership category.

As the business and management domain comes to define leadership and 'own' the leadership discourse, so too is facilitated 'the development of a coherent system of management control' (Knights and Morgan 1992). The discourse around leaders, such as corporate executives, is correspondingly impoverished. Their 'visions' end up being narrowly framed around corporate earning power or expansion plans. Management-fashioned profiles of leaders describe them taking corporate risks but not, by and large, psychic risks.

For all these reasons, the business definition of leadership as the solitary, out-front hero leading the troops into battle is a very seductive one. However, it encourages us to dwell on a one-dimensional set of performances which are becoming increasingly anachronistic in a diverse workplace and international market. It also encourages us to see the leader outside of her or his history and group, to inflate their powers and potency to fix things (Meindl, Ehrlich and Dukerich 1985).

Economic imperatives and business ideologies

Most researchers agree that the development of multiculturalism in the 1970s signalled an important shift—in public policy at least—towards recognition rather than denial of difference, and acknowledgement of the value diversity brings to society. Yet the mythologies of egalitarianism run deep, and they form a connection with the new business ideology. This ideology of competitive individualism casts individuals as the great heroes who will be liberated to economic achievement by free, global competition. In this view, government's job is not to protect the disadvantaged but to dismantle barriers to competition and to cut regulatory and other 'unnecessary' costs of doing business. As Sinclair has argued elsewhere (1994; 1998), ideas about leadership in the business arena reflect the values and heroes of local mythology. Despite the evidence that stratification and segregation continue to separate corporate elites from the rest of society, business leaders generally hold onto the view that merit prevails as the only determinant of who becomes a leader. There is a widespread view that discrimination doesn't happen and that prejudice has disappeared from the rational, hard-headed domain of corporate life.

While our research has focused on how leaders brought their experiences and advocacy of difference into their organisations, it was clear that executives were operating within constraints that were not set by companies alone but by broader macro-economic trends and changing ideologies about how business should respond to new challenges. Framing leaders' perceptions of what they could do, and had done, were organisational 'imperatives'— most commonly pressures for growth and internationalisation, simultaneous pressures to downsize or do more with fewer employees, organisational change initiatives and restructuring with a variety of objectives, and pressures to exploit opportunities from electronic commerce, such as building electronically implemented alliances.

These external pressures are complex in their effects. Many broad trends contain both positive and negative potential for a different kind of leadership. For example, the reduced barriers and increased international opportunities for business that are part of internationalisation have provided incentives for business to manage differences well and to include cross-cultural competencies among leaders' skills. At the same time companies exhibit conservatism and ethnocentrism in defining which cross-cultural differences will continue to be important and how business should differentiate and standardise in its response. Contrary to predictions that reduced geographical barriers and heightened communications would elicit 'seamless' international operation, business cultures are not becoming more alike. Rather, local or tribal differences have often become more pronounced as other aspects of corporate life become more standardised. For some companies, 'internationalising' has been an opportunity to outsource aspects of production while remaining resolutely culture-centric and homogeneous in the management of their operations.

Workplace trends such as restructuring and technological innovation also contain both positive and negative potential for openness to difference. A number of interviewees saw that pressures on companies to become more competitive through restructuring introduced opportunities to innovate, to outsource and contract in, as well as to appoint new, often younger and different, talent to middle and senior positions. This interviewee cited an 'outcomes' focus, technological innovation and project management as reasons why his organisation was inadvertently utilising a broader talent pool:

> We're moving to more project management approaches across traditional functional areas. So you need a greater mix of types of people and competencies. That has a greater impact than things like [diversity] training programs because you focus on skills and competencies . . . It's a hidden benefit of what some technical issues like Y2K have done for us . . . You may be dealing with someone you never see. When visibility is less, you focus more on outcomes than whether the person you're dealing with is old or young or black or whatever.

The same trends that reduce barriers and create competition have also promoted an emphasis on individualism and market-based solutions in workplaces. A strong value on self-help and self-reliance can tend to ignore issues of systemic disadvantage. In organisations, increased opportunities for some, accompanied with fewer traditional protective mechanisms, have translated into more atomised workplace cultures where it's 'every person for themselves' (Sennett 1998). Some of the features of this workplace culture include:

- rationalising, restructuring and downsizing which cuts any slack from the system and expects one employee to do what used to be the work of several;
- expanding the hours of work regarded as essential, particularly among professional and managerial personnel;
- a switch to contract-based employment, including shorter-term and highly-specified work to be delivered;
- paring back benefits provided by employers and a general trend to shorter periods of employment;
- a climate of 'smaller' government, lower regulatory intervention in the area of equal employment opportunity and an emphasis on industry self-regulation.

These features of the new workplace culture have significant ramifications for openness to differences, for risk-taking and for trialling new initiatives. Managers working long hours and feeling stressed have few incentives to look beyond the next reporting cycle in order to think about strategic investment in diversity capital. Within tightly monitored performance systems, what doesn't get measured doesn't get done. Sennett argues that the regime of exercising control via performance targets appears to offer flexibility in how those targets are met. Yet in effect it provides a 'specious freedom' because targets far exceed capabilities. The evidence that managers are overburdened helps explain our finding that while they are aware of the benefits of diversity, they are unable to act. Managerial overburdening adds to an existing economics of inequality, Sennett argues, creating 'new forms of unequal, arbitrary power within the organization' (1998: 55).

A second set of consequences flowing from these trends in workplace culture concern how discrimination is viewed. In the perfectly competitive market, discrimination is driven out by individual consumers, employees and shareholders exercising rational preferences. Despite recognition that this ideal is never realised in practice, the individualisation of the relationship between employer and employee assumes that all employees are equally well equipped to defend their performance, their record and their rights. As Ian Watson (1996) revealed in his study of 'the glass door', this 'survival of the fittest' mentality puts at a distinct disadvantage those prospective employees without the same 'cultural capital' as their employers.

A highly pressured and insecure work environment can also leave managers focusing on fending for themselves and perhaps their immediate work group. Insecurity creates fear and a retreat to the familiar (Reynolds 2001). Under these circumstances, managers close ranks around those who are trusted as being like themselves. People who are judged as different or outsiders in this regime are often scapegoated as a means for the in-group to feel safer. The dynamics of resisting and attacking what is different are well-documented responses among people feeling threatened themselves (Cox 1993; Australian Psychological Society 1997).

In many industrialised countries, there is a trend to 'smaller government' and in areas such as equal employment opportunity, legislation is being wound back. For example, in Australia the

Affirmative Action Act (1986) has been replaced by the *Equal Employment Opportunity for Women in the Workplace Act* (1999). The Act was re-titled partially to avoid the offence caused when business falsely interpreted affirmative action in the Australian context to mean government-imposed quotas for the hiring of members of minority groups (Sinclair 2000). As well as being re-titled in a less threatening manner, the new Act is explicitly set up to reduce costs of compliance. It requires companies to report less often about their EEO policies and practices, and introduces no serious sanctions on companies that don't comply.

The argument accompanying these changes is that the market will drive irrational discriminatory practices out of the system. Competitive pressures will ensure companies seek to recruit and develop the best possible talent, regardless of individuals' cultural and racial backgrounds.

Yet the evidence is that companies are not perfectly responsive to market pressures. They persist with traditional approaches, not because these make logical or economic good sense, but because they are more comfortable and familiar with such approaches. Although it is a widely shared contemporary wisdom that regulation doesn't work in changing behaviours and that it is better to encourage business to build its own case for being open and non-discriminatory, the evidence is much more mixed. Conducting a review of Affirmative Action, for example, Linnehan and Konrad (1999) find that such legislation has, in many countries, delivered significant improvements in the opportunities available to, and representation of, minority groups in organisations.

Unless organisations actively recognise and reward their managers for recruiting and developing a diverse range of employees, and for valuing and rewarding openness to difference, then these issues can become a matter of unthinking neglect, a low priority that rarely registers on the managerial horizon—unless a crisis such as a discrimination action, arrests leadership attention. Managing difference better requires prioritisation, extra effort, a strategic approach and an eye for the longer term. Given the current context, these are unlikely to occur unless there is a strong mandate or overriding organisational imperative.

Multicultural society and monocultural leadership

Australia is now one of the world's most multicultural societies. In the last fifty years Australia's immigration program has been larger than that of any other country except Israel. This emphasis on immigration, and our burgeoning international higher education market, mean that business can recruit from an incomparably diverse and well-educated graduate pool. For example, overseas-born chemical engineers and electrical engineers made up 49 per cent and 48 per cent respectively of the total degree-qualified workforce (Birrell and Hawthorne 1997).

Further, statistics show Australia is also distinctive among nations for the very high rates of inter-marriage among various ethnic groups and comparatively low levels of inter-racial tension.

While Australia is known for its multiculturalism, for sponsoring a climate in which immigrants have achieved a great deal, Australian business presents a paradox. Despite the large and multicultural managerial talent pool, the evidence is that Australian companies have been slow to recruit and then promote and develop that talent into leadership in large corporates. Corporate leadership is characterised by a remarkable homogeneity in cultural and gender terms. Among Australian CEOs, directors and senior executives, strong but tacit expectations have produced a group with little diversity in cultural and gender characteristics. Myths of egalitarianism and tolerance enshrined in the cultural psyche have allowed us to pretend that racism and prejudice don't apply to most parts of society, including business.

Historians and other researchers have shown that the picture of Australia as an egalitarian, open and inclusive society, in which people of all backgrounds have equal opportunities to achieve, is more mythology than reality. Australia is, and has always been, a stratified and segregated society. This is evidenced by the continuing obstacles to various people who, though well-qualified and able, are not assuming leadership roles in numbers consistent with their presence and contribution to our community. For example, only 8 per cent of Federal members of Parliament elected in 1998 were from a non-English-speaking immigrant background. This is despite that group being 23 per cent of the population and at least as well educated as the Australian-born population, and a history of fifty years of substantial immigration (Cope and Kalantzis 2000). Professionals from immigrant backgrounds, particularly those who are non-English-speaking, continue to face explicit and implicit discriminatory obstacles in having their skills and contribution recognised.

Turning to corporate leadership, researchers have shown that the senior executives and directors of Australian companies reflect only the narrowest slice of Australian society, with few women, few born in non-English-speaking or Asian countries and no Aboriginal representation. This group brings a narrow range of experiences, values and perspectives to the task of corporate leadership: it is monocultural leadership for a multicultural society.

In addition, and as documented in Chapter 5, there have been very strong pressures arising from the prevalent business and economic ideology to camouflage rather than celebrate differences, to conform to a traditional narrow heroic template of leadership which can only be exhibited by and recognised in a small elite of monocultural men.

The history of Australia is one in which the contribution to development and commerce by people of non-Anglo background has not been, and still is not, widely recognised. Although there is an extensive history of migration to Australia, the White Australia policy was not dismantled until the 1970s. Until the Second World War, official statistics and histories perpetuated the deception that Australia was an egalitarian democracy created from a racially homogeneous society. Elaine Thompson points out the irony of this position: 'Australia's special cultural characteristic was its egalitarian spirit and that spirit was best protected and nurtured through the idea of a single homogeneous race' (1994: 81). Until comparatively recently, a good deal of Australia's energies, in official policy and though other cultural mechanisms, were aimed at minimising cultural and racial diversity. Kalantzis *et al.* (1993) show that the popular myths enshrined in one reading of Australian history—the mateship, 'fair go' and egalitarianism—have only ever referred to and included privileged groups, and typically not immigrants, women and indigenous peoples. As

Manning Clark wrote in *A History of Australia*, 'Mateship was the mythology of a tribe who loved men of their own kind, while entertaining the most savage hatreds against all strangers, all new-comers, all coloured peoples, Aborigines, natives of the islands of the Pacific, Englishmen, Jews' (1981: 56)

Australia's 200-year attachment to the mythology of egalitarian-ism has, according to Thompson (1994) further entrenched dis-crimination, promoting the denial of immigrant and indigenous experience, delays in public policy responses and a tendency to 'blame the victim'—to dismiss poverty, unemployment, illiteracy as the problems of individuals who failed to make an effort. She concludes that a paradox underpins Australia's attitude to dif-ference: 'Australia was egalitarian *because* it was xenophobic and sexist. White Australia was the direct product of an Australian egalitarianism based around the central egalitarian idea of *same-ness*—that its society was socially and culturally homogeneous and that such homogeneity was an indispensable precondition of democracy' (Thompson 1994: 252). In this context, postwar immigration was embraced because of the confident expectation of assimilation.

Profound changes have occurred in immigration over the last fifty years in Australia, yet it is a field in which stereotypes con-tinued to prevail about the scale of migration and the qualifi-cations of immigrants. For example, the stereotype for migrant women is of peasant origins, few professional and educational qualifications and an employment record in Australia in unskilled or semi-skilled work in manufacturing and service sectors. In fact, statistics from the late 1980s onwards show male and female immigrants from the Asian region to be twice or three times more likely than their local counterparts to have professional training. Asian female migrants were also much less likely than local women or than migrants from the UK and Europe to have left school by sixteen. The data on the qualifications of migrant women were particularly distorted until recently. Large numbers of female engineers, economists, accountants and other pro-fessionals were listed as 'home duties' simply because they were listed as wives of 'principal applicants' and their occupations were accordingly not recorded (Hawthorne 1996; see also Jayasuriya and Kee, 1999. Mighty (1997) shows a similar pattern in Canada of immigrant women being much more highly educated and qualified than locals).

Turning to the experiences of Aboriginal Australians, Henry Reynolds (1999) argues that the Australian mythology of egalitarianism and the celebration of frontier achievement was made possible by a deeply embedded racism. Historians were able to preserve these mythologies simply by removing our relations with Australia's original inhabitants from official history, and by not counting Aboriginals as fully human when battles with white settlers yielded enormous loss of Aboriginal lives.

Australians and the recorders of Australian history have thus used a variety of devices to perpetuate a view of Australia as egalitarian and free of racism. Underlying an ostensible openness was a deep distrust of, and discomfort with, many cultural and racial differences. This cultural portrayal and what lies behind it are, of course, not just historical artefacts. Continuing debates about reconciliation with Aboriginal peoples; about population, immigration and refugees; and about military defence, alliances and protection, reflect a contemporary reluctance to face racism—co-existent with erecting and policing the borders of a traditional, perhaps vanishing, Australian identity.

Some critics also argue that official policies like multiculturalism have allowed us to hide behind the seductive idea of our own 'tolerance'. For example, Ghassan Hage (1998) argues that most of what passes as 'multiculturalism' and multicultural tolerance simply reinforces existing power structures: a mode of domination is presented as a form of egalitarianism. The discourse of tolerance urges those with the power of intolerance to simply not exercise it, rather than to challenge and change the underlying power structures which create the tolerators and tolerated. Proponents of these views critique the simple focus on 'celebrating' or 'managing' differences which fails to recognise the power dynamics by which difference is identified and labelled. Hage also suggests that our public policy flirtation with the glamorous side of diversity management has enabled us to feel complacent while overlooking the structural inequities that characterise multiculturalism. In her book *No Logo* Naomi Klein argues that diversity has become a tool of the marketers, a 'candy-coated multiculturalism' which is used as a cure-all for the pitfalls of global expansion (2000: 117). According to Iris Young (1990), a politics of difference will promote social justice only when it prevents dominant social groups from treating their norms and privilege as neutral and universal, against which others are judged as 'minorities' or 'different'.

Australian organisations and corporate leaders thus operate within a wider cultural and social context which promotes assumptions of egalitarianism while denying evidence of systemic racism and structural inequalities for those from non-English speaking backgrounds. These cultural myths form a potent backdrop, providing strong disincentives to corporate and business leaders who might advocate the value of differences to organisations. Issues of discrimination or racism become taboo, and any leader who voices concerns about these issues risks his or her belonging to the corporate elite.

A wider understanding of what leaders need

Differences continue to be salient in the ways workers want to work, how communities live and what they value. The need to appreciate and respond to cultural differences remains a crucial ingredient of success, whether it be in running operations, or in marketing and supplying to people in diverse and niche markets. Recognition of the need to differentiate products and services and match the demographies of markets with diversity inside organisations has often been belated and grudging. 'Even underwear has national characteristics' lamented the head of Sara Lee, after his company struggled to adapt its products to critically important local requirements. The evidence is that, in the business world at least, leadership which embraces and endorses differences, remains a rare thing.

Critics have argued that the corporate cultures which are purportedly global and uniformly embraced in far-flung parts of the world are often simply the new face of imperialism. In this view the 'global strategy' of many large multinationals is one dominant home country culture imposing itself in diverse operating and market environments with little capacity or serious willingness to adapt its business practices, let alone learn from the locals. These forms of neo-colonialism use new tools and new discourses to justify their ambitions, but they are not so very different in the structures of asymmetrical power that underpin them and in their irrevocable effects on local business economies, cultures and societies (Prasad 1997; Wong-Ming Ji and Mir 1997).

Commentators have also noted that transnational companies have the power and resources that, increasingly, governments don't have. In their analysis of organisational violence Hearn and Parkin note that '(O)f the 100 largest economies, half are corporations, half are countries' (2001: 127). The concentration of corporate power, along with the transcending of traditional boundaries, creates new possibilities for violations and oppressions which are complex, hidden and unable to be monitored or controlled.

In many industrialised and developing countries, governments are vacating domains they have traditionally regulated, and increasing their expectations on companies to self-regulate and establish appropriate standards—in areas from worker health and safety to advertising standards. In many less developed parts of the world, because of their central role in domestic economies, companies come to occupy quasi-government roles. Large corporations set standards, they help to establish laws and they fund and support regulation and monitoring. They train local managers in technologies and business practices, mentoring local leadership elites.

Organisations are now routinely recruiting highly qualified graduates who are demographically diverse in terms of their cultural and racial makeup. Building managerial capability from this highly diverse base also represents a new leadership challenge in itself. And it is a challenge few organisations meet well, as promotion systems end up delivering at a leadership level a group which is far narrower and more homogeneous than the talent pool. Continuing reliance on an expatriate workforce to lead international subsidiaries is another reflection of corporate preference for homogeneity and consistency in leadership styles.

These changes in the environment and expectations of corporations create not just strategic and commercial opportunities but also new moral challenges for leaders. They are no longer simply managers conversant with business practices; these contexts require diplomats, willing and able to appreciate how business intermeshes with broader social and cultural practices, and negotiators who are able to operationalise complex and sometimes fragile structures. Companies are a force for change, whatever they do, but their leaders (sometimes inadvertently) have the impacts of statesmen and stateswomen—with significant economic, social and in some cases political, ramifications.

In this wider moral environment, what sort of leadership is needed? In some respects it is easier to define what we don't want: leaders with narrow experiences; those who are part of a closed or insular elite; those who have only ever seen and experienced a privileged slice of life, who believe that their own way is the best way, or worse, the only way. In effect, this is all too often the profile of leaders that companies have traditionally selected, rewarded and elevated to leadership—executives chosen from elite schools and universities, on a managed 'high potential' path through key organisational roles and spending much of their career in one organisation.

Homogeneity of leadership in itself also has the potential to be destructive, if not evil. Studies of the preconditions of disaster indicate that homogeneous decision-making groups are prone to disregard warning signs, to develop illusions of grandiosity and invincibility, to believe themselves to be above normal rules. Equally, whistleblowers who signal significant corporate wrongdoing are likely to be on the edge of, or outside, the dominant group. From a moral or corporate governance point of view, diversity in the backgrounds and perspectives of senior managers can provide a valuable safeguard.

Several decades ago, William Whyte warned of the dangers of the organisation man (1959). Michael Maccoby also documented the company man in his analysis of organisational types, and he has followed this with a profile of the narcissistic leader (2000). In his in-depth study Robert Jackall (1988) documented the moral consequences of organisations having been built on traditional corporate cultures in which blame was pushed down, credit pushed up and obsessive fealty to the top was the overwhelming guiding principle. The risks are that traditional organisational cultures reinforce and reward leadership of a narrow kind—built on limited experience, unused to respecting and adapting to important differences, sceptical of the validity of disadvantage or discrimination because it has never been felt at first hand.

We have argued that in this new environment we need a different recipe for leadership. We need leaders who have:

- ways of putting their own values in context, reflecting on how those values have come about and how they shape and limit leadership practice;
- well-practised habits of being able to hear and recognise the validity of different ways of looking at and experiencing the world;
- identities which do not rest on membership of a single social group or tribe but are able to inhabit multiple groups and cultures without feeling threatened or paralysed;
- courage to stand up to the status quo, and argue for and practice a different way of doing things.

Ways of leading in the new corporate world

Despite the presence of global brands and universal technologies, the business world continues to be challenged by differences. Successful, sustainable companies are those which understand these differences, utilising them in their operations and responding to them in the goods and services they provide as well as how they continually re-make themselves in a dynamic market.

The requirement on business to 'manage' differences will mean many different things in practice. Managing difference well will not mean subsuming differences, or assimilating them, tolerating or even accommodating them. Rather, the new requirement will be to develop organisations in which differences are everywhere and infuse the organisation with vigour and complexity, robustness and flexibility. It will mean developing the capacity to nurture multiple cultures and subcultures in the organisation, rather than imposing a single dominant corporate culture (Sinclair 1991). In these organisations where differences flourish, the integrative task of leaders becomes even more important. What are the capabilities they need? Or, more profoundly, who might they be?

There is a substantial and expanding literature on the emerging skills of globalism(Bartlett and Ghoshal 2002). But to understand how people work with and lead difference, we need more than a focus on global skills or cross-cultural behaviours. In this book we have argued the need to take a much wider and deeper perspective than most business and management texts allow. A wider perspective takes into account the structural changes in societies and business surrounding corporate leadership. As governments retract their roles and corporations become as powerful as old nation states, business leaders face new moral challenges but are equipped with a business ideology that is often impoverished and imprisoning.

A deeper perspective shows that it is often individual 'roots' in childhood and 'routes' through early career and organisations that provide the best clues to an individual leader's stance towards difference. Ultimately our discussion needs to encompass issues of identity and the construction of identities which are rooted in multiple cultures. It is to these issues we turn in this concluding chapter.

We started this book with profiles of two of our interviewees to show how leaders from radically different backgrounds are taking their experiences of border-crossing into their leadership. We start the final chapter with two examples taken from the popular press that contrast the traditional expectations and values of leadership from those we argue are emerging.

The first example is of Jac Nasser, Lebanese-born but brought up in Australia, recently retired CEO of Ford worldwide. In an article in the business press, assorted experts comment on his leadership style:

> 'a real blood and guts, balls-out guy. He doesn't take any crap from anybody, whether it is the Ford family or anyone else'; 'He basically works seven 15-hour days'; 'a fine executive' with 'a bare-knuckles style of management'; 'a legendary steel plated tough guy' who, on his own admission knows 'how to get through tough times' (Riley 2001).

The Ford Car Company, under Nasser's leadership, weathered multiple challenges: law suits and class actions, major recalls of its products. And there are many possible explanations for Nasser's rise to power and subsequent departure from the CEO's job. But our desire in this research has been to look beneath the construction of this kind of leadership and ask whether it is increasingly ill-suited to the challenges of contemporary organisations. The question for us is not Can this leader endure and therefore succeed? but Why do we construct leadership as this kind of triumph?

There is little doubt that studies and stories of corporate leadership over the past several decades have been dominated by the tough-guy template (Sinclair 1998). Typical 'profiles' of leaders in the corporate press laud self-reliance and toughness as the essence of leadership, without asking from where this template comes, whose interests it advances and what it leaves out. We argue that traditional approaches to leadership that value the outfront, solitary and self-reliant hero are drastically inappropriate to the complex business context described in Chapter 6.

Our other example is Dr Condoleeza Rice, national security adviser to President Bush, also black and female. A cousin of Rice describes her upbringing: 'Condi and I speak the King's English to the Queen's taste. We're fluent in all kinds of white cultures. We float right through them. But there are very few interracially fluent whites.' Condi Rice herself is reported as seeing this less in terms of race than strategic thinking. 'I'm not naïve' she says, 'I know that race is a factor, and I know that racism is a factor. But I've always thought once you've said that, where does it leave you? You need a strategy to deal with it.' (Russakoff 2001)

These two examples—Jac Nasser and Condi Rice—are not offered as examples of old or new, effective or ineffective, leadership. However, the discussion of leadership that often accompanies high profile leaders such as these raises questions raises about the traditional templates of toughness. We find themes which are indicative of the new faces of leadership. The experiences of people such as Rice, and the 'interracial fluency' that often flows from these experiences are the new requisites for leaders.

Transcultural competence and multicultural identities

Various metaphors and constructs have been deployed by researchers working in areas of international business, cross-cultural and diversity management. Robert Rosen, for example (2000), argues the case for 'global literacies'. Global literacies are in turn grounded in personal and cultural literacies. By this Rosen means that understanding and valuing yourself is the bedrock for cultural literacies, or knowing and leveraging cultural differences in business contexts. The literacy metaphor conveys a picture of leaders being fluent in many business languages, conversant in noticing and adapting to the business norms of different societies. The pinnacle of development in some models of transnationalism is that stage where race, or culture, or one's 'native' language disappears, leaving no preferences for working in one cultural domain rather than another, but rather a capacity for seamless skills and comfort.

Emerging from substantial cross-cultural research has been the notion of 'intercultural competence' or 'the ability to communicate effectively in cross-cultural situations and to relate appropriately in a variety of cultural contexts' (Bennett and Bennett 2001). Intercultural competence has two components: a 'heartset' to do with attitudes and knowledge, and a 'skillset' to do with behaviours. The intercultural 'mindset' or 'heartset' includes cultural self-awareness, frameworks for creating cultural contrasts (such as understandings about communication styles), a capacity to use cultural generalisations without stereotyping and, finally, the maintenance of motivators for working with difference such as curiosity and tolerance for ambiguity. Intercultural competence also includes an intercultural 'skillset' which is the ability to analyse interactions and to adapt and expand behaviours to respond to different situations. In this understanding of intercultural competence, knowledge, behaviour and attitude work together or move in tandem. It is not possible to demonstrate competence with the knowledge but no skills, and vice versa. In his research on transitions, Adams (1976) shows how making physical or geographical transitions—learning how to live and work in a culturally different place—fosters greater adaptability and a stronger, more robust sense of self.

Fons Trompenaars and Charles Hampden-Turner advance the concept of 'transcultural competence', which they see as 'a new capacity for bridging business differences' (2002: 14). It involves three steps of recognising (not denying), respecting (not devaluing or ignoring) and actively reconciling differences. This new business competence, they argue, goes beyond 'either-or' thinking and even 'and-and' thinking to create a new coherence which contains seemingly opposed values. Step one of recognition involves under-standing differences—such as knowing the difference between a highly particularistic versus a universalistic culture. Transcultural competence involves having a sophisticated stereotype, noticing the trouble it causes and the way exceptions occur, and then moving beyond it. Step three of actively reconciling involves finding the place where two opposites meet or can coexist. An example is applying universal rules but also allowing exceptions: 'a transculturally competent leader can make a virtuous circle of rule making and exception finding' (2002: 24). Logical, sensible excep-tions simply make the universal rules stronger and more robust. 'The transculturally competent know that individualism versus communitarianism is a false dichotomy. The real art is to nurture individuals . . . so that they can serve groups' (2002: 35) and, we might add, to nurture groups so that they can serve individuals.

These models of intercultural and transcultural competency take us beyond metaphors of fluency and literacy. They focus on ways of conceptualising opportunities, ways of solving problems and decision-making that become manifest in managerial action. Through our research we argue the need to broaden still further—to ways of being. Our perspective has been to build a picture of the leader—who they are and where they have come from—because we believe that these experiences are an important com-ponent of how any leader deals with difference.

In the race literature there is a tradition of research on more deeply embedded constructs of identity. Initially this was con-cerned with the identity experiences of minority groups in a white-dominated society. It is not surprising that this would be so, because historically white identity has not been problematised but regarded as the norm around which minority groups have had to assimilate and adapt. As we discussed in Chapter 5, experiences of bi-culturalism, or moving in and out of more than one culture, are common for those from a minority background working in white-dominated organisations. These writers, however, note that bi-culturalism can come with some costs. For example, for blacks operating in a predominantly white environment, there may be costs associated with actively suppressing parts of self (Bell and Nkomo 2001). There might be a much higher emotional cost on some who move across several cultural groups as they negotiate and re-negotiate their belonging and 'credentials' to be part of that group.

Recent research has revealed the power dynamics that construct and conceal white racial identity (Helms 1990; Bowser and Hunt 1996). All of us have a racial identity—it is just that some have the luxury of assuming its legitimacy and never having to defend it or camouflage it in order to succeed. Postmodern researchers maintain that none of us has a fixed identity. The idea of a single, stable and coherent self that we as individuals work to create and shape is a fiction arising from a narcissistic age. The scope that we have to develop and express sides of our identities will be dramatically constrained and limited by structural factors, economic opportunities, expectations that societies have for members of racial, cultural or gender groups.

People with a bicultural or transcultural identity may feel relatively comfortable moving across and being part of several distinctive cultural domains. But this fluidity may also carry with it a sense of impaired or compromised belonging or a sense of not being fully accepted and at home in any place. Our research has shown that those whose identities are rooted in multiple cultures experience both ease and discomfort. The leaders we have studied experience the bi-cultural facility that comes from inhabiting several cultures, but they also experience the discomfort that comes from never quite belonging closely. This provides a sense of perspective on self and a sense of outsider-ness or other-ness that is at the heart of the reflective leadership that is our focus. So, in contrast to research that conceptualises a kind of seamless comfort in many cultures, for us the hallmark of the reflective leader of difference is the varying and constant re-positioning of self, the experiences of comfort and discomfort, sensitivity and openness to learning and acting differently, that can flow from these experiences.

Putting backgrounds back into leadership

It doesn't seem such a radical idea to argue that people's backgrounds—childhoods, families, early career—might be important ingredients in the leaders that they become. Yet it is a very uncommon emphasis in the management and leadership literature which more often takes the leader as a 'given' and sets about 'topping' him or her 'up' with the latest in leadership skills and knowledge—whether they be emotional intelligence or techniques of balanced scorecard reporting.

Analysis of personal backgrounds is often rejected, with some justification, as being overly deterministic: condemning or applauding the person on the basis of circumstances which happened to them rather than recognising the role of individual determination and ability in shaping what they become. It is important to emphasise that the events themselves don't create the leader. We are not saying that unless you've had a border-crossing experience, for example, you won't have what is needed for leadership. Rather, it is what the leader makes of these experiences that is critical.

Further, if organisations want to build these new leadership capabilities they may well want to put a new value on experiences in crossing borders and managing differences. Although this may mean placing different emphases in their recruitment and promotion, it may also mean encouraging existing managers to look again at their own backgrounds and to build new learning from a fresh understanding of their own experiences and how it has shaped who they are. The leadership we are describing here is not static but is always work-in-progress. Gaining new insights from analysing one's past actions and understanding better the impinging constraints and opportunities is the stuff of leadership learning itself. We argue that in leaving backgrounds out of the picture, much of traditional leadership development work ignores a vital and rich repository of learning.

Roots and routes

Our analysis of thirty leaders has focused on those we have described as 'outsiders moving in' and 'insiders moving out'. Despite their different circumstances there are themes in the backgrounds of leaders across both groups. Taking family contexts first, these leaders are likely to be second- or later-born in large families. As family psychologists show, every child has a different experience of the same family. From the child's point of view, these differences can be so great that it can feel like the first- and second-born inhabit different families. We postulate that later-borns, and particularly those in large or extended families, have opportunities to develop skills of empathy and negotiation earlier, because they have to. Unlike first-borns, they can't rely on their position in the family to get what they want. Instead, there is an early experience of having to recognise and work with different siblings and family members. This self-reliance was intensified in the case of some of our leaders with absent fathers. While many imbided strong values of hard work and education from their father's model, others found the space to be different through paternal absence.

The second theme shared in our leaders' experiences was a change in physical boundaries, often during the key years of ado-lescence. Migration, exposure to multiple cultures, dislocation, being a newcomer or an outsider, were all part of their growing up or early career. Their experiences of crossing physical and less tan-gible borders provided the bases for rich learning about self and others. Crossing borders throws one's own values and assump-tions into sharp relief. The experience stimulates the capacity to read and attune to subtle cultural differences. Being an outsider or newcomer also reveals patterns of status and hierarchy that are invisible to the insider. Finally, these experiences can include being on the receiving end of racism or discrimination, which can mobilise a strong sense of social justice and commitment to equality without regard to first language or skin colour.

The third chapter focused on the routes taken by our insiders and outsiders through early career to leadership. We drew on research from psychologists, educationalists and others to tease out the origins of qualities which are at the heart of the leadership described here: openness to others, the capacity to trust, flexibility of one's own boundaries and a preparedness to challenge.

The organisational shape of the leadership that emerges from these experiences is described in Chapter 4. It consists of inter-linking ingredients, capabilities and strategies. In the attunement to others and practices of listening and learning from others, we argue that this leadership is fundamentally different in its orientation to traditional techniques of command and control. Driving these different strategies is a comfort in one's own skin and comfort with those at all levels of organisations, an identification with the underdog that grows out of personal experiences of 'outsiderness' and a courage to challenge unfairness and injustice.

Chapters 5 and 6 turned from the individual makeup of leaders to the context in which leadership sits. Here, we outlined some of the many reasons why conservative and traditional approaches to leadership persist; why leaders do not differentiate themselves from a leadership elite and why they are generally reticent to advocate or identify themselves with the interests of ethnic or cultural constituencies in leadership.

Despite our desires and indeed the prescriptions which define leadership by its transforming power, leadership often remains a conservative force in society. To understand the reasons for this we need to look at broader Australian society, including the myths such as egalitarianism which sustain it. We also need to look at the effects of current dominant business ideologies which tend to neglect systemic and structural sources of disadvantage and vest hopes in free markets and open competition as the means to remove inequities and irrational barriers in the way that organisations are staffed, managed and led. It is important to comprehend the full force of these obstacles to appreciate why new faces of leadership might be slow to emerge.

We cannot move to new forms of leadership without understanding the array of historic and structural, institutional and individual pressures which tie us to traditional models. These are significant brakes on the emergence and validation of new forms of leading. Yet new faces of corporate leadership are emerging. Our wish is that this research has demonstrated in more depth and richness the value of different kinds of life experience to the new territories and tasks of leadership.

APPENDIX

The Research Process

This book is based around a core piece of research conducted during 1999 and 2000. It formed part of a project organised by the Department of Immigration and Multicultural Affairs (DIMA). The project—called the Productive Diversity Partnerships Program —was designed to bring together management education institutions around Australia to conduct a variety of research projects exploring 'productive diversity'. The underlying belief was that support for multiculturalism in the business context must come from those responsible for educating the managers of the future. DIMA provided a framework within which management and business academics, researchers and consultants would undertake various research projects in productive diversity, which would then inform the development of public policy and promote advances in management education in the areas of diversity.

Research groups used a range of methods, including case studies of organisations, large-scale statistical surveys and the development and piloting of diversity 'tools'. Each team shared their findings at workshops before the culmination of the process—a conference in Melbourne in November 2000 entitled: '21st Century Business: Delivering the Diversity Dividend', attended by business leaders, human resources managers, bureaucrats and academics from Australia and overseas.

While DIMA's sponsorship was a catalyst for this research, our interest in leadership and cross-cultural issues, as well as a shared commitment to qualitative research methods, goes back much further. Both of us have been trained and are experienced as in-depth interviewers. We had worked together previously, including on diversity projects, where we had come to realise the complexity and sensitivity of working in areas of difference. These experiences instilled a commitment to go deeper in our own work in diversity. We believed that real attitudes towards diversity would not be readily or usefully captured by larger sample, questionnaire-type data gathering. We needed to hear and respect peoples' experiences. We needed to be brave in tackling difficult and painful experiences.

Our project methodology was therefore qualitative. The plan was to conduct discursive, narrative interviews to explore ideas about leadership and about diversity. More unusually, we wanted to explore childhoods and early experiences to see what relevance, if any, there was for current business/leadership practice. We decided that our initial sample would consist of Anglo-Celtic business leaders who were known to have some particular interest in workplace diversity, or who were known to be reflective about the issues. This sample profile was selected because we wanted to explore the notion 'diversity leadership' as a set of practices that all leaders could develop regardless of their own ethnicity, gender and background. We also regarded our research as a catalyst for promoting reflection and discussion about diversity among senior executives; it was important to target those who, we believed, had the power and capacity to take a leadership role on these issues. We set about identifying people for this sample using established networks of contacts in business circles. With only one or two exceptions, the people we contacted were happy to participate. The few refusals were politely ascribed to business priorities—itself an important insight into how diversity was positioned in these businesses. For the rest, there was a quite surprising, and reassuring, willingness to be involved.

Drawing on research, we developed an outline of the interview schedule. This was used as a prompt and to ensure we covered all the areas we were interested in. But we were also very committed to, and experienced in, following the interviewees' narratives, 'hearing' in the fullest sense their experiences, and probing their most salient experiences and ideas around difference. The interview schedule was a checklist rather than a map for the interview and we found that interviewees pursued their own unique course while still covering the territory in which we were interested. The three areas we sought to cover were:

- Personal understandings and experiences of difference and diversity, including families, growing up, education and early career. Experiences of difference, such as cross-culturalism in childhood; experiences of being an outsider themselves; how they remembered differences being understood and portrayed in the family and childhood contexts.
- Exploration of critical incidents of managing difference in the workplace, including those judged effective and those judged less successful.
- Observations about the characteristics of organisations and industries which, in the interviewee's experience, were open to differences, and those which were more closed and posed challenges for managing diversity.

Having arranged interviews, we sent an advance letter flagging broadly the three areas we would be interested in exploring. We did this knowing that our first area of interest—childhood and personal background—was not territory in which they were accustomed to being interviewed, especially by people coming from a business school environment. When the Department of Immigration received our initial report it would be fair to say that they seemed a little surprised at the personal depth of response that our work had uncovered.

Nevertheless, it was sufficiently well received for us to be asked to extend the research and conduct a second phase. Phase 2 involved another sample of corporate leaders, but this time born in non-English speaking countries. This raised far greater difficulty in sample identification. Where were these overseas-born, non-English-as-first-language leaders? There were several very high profile overseas-born business leaders who had started their own companies and gone on to great success. There were also many overseas-born success stories in public sector leadership roles. Among long-standing, large corporations, however, there seemed to be very few non-English-speaking-origin migrants in leadership ranks. Again, this was an important finding in itself.

There was also a dearth of networks, or even registers, to identify such people. We asked organisations such as Asialink and the Multicultural Affairs Foundation, who were very helpful. But it was for them, as for us, a matter of rifling through card indexes and general business directories and making phone calls until we finally gathered together sufficient numbers for our sample. This process turned out to be symptomatic of one of our main findings about corporate leaders from different backgrounds and what they 'do' with their difference. Firstly, in mainstream corporate Australia there are relatively few leaders from these backgrounds. Secondly, those that do exist either have lower public profiles or actually seek to minimise or hide their difference.

We conducted a total of thirty interviews, each lasting an average of sixty to ninety minutes. For both samples our methodology was the same. We wrote letters of introduction about ourselves and our research project. We made interview times, usually asking for about one hour. Though most thought an hour a rather long time to set aside, in many cases it was our interviewees who extended well over the initial deadline! All but one interview was con- ducted in person in Melbourne or Sydney; the remaining one was via conference call to Perth.

We conducted roughly half the interviews each, immediately doing full verbatim transcripts of our respective interviews so that we could read each other's interviews promptly. The process of doing one's own verbatim transcripts is in itself a powerful research tool. It requires that one re-live the interview in a particu- larly painstaking and time-consuming way, poring over each word in a tape-recording, hearing once again not just words, but lan- guage, tone, nuance, hesitation, silence and so on. In our experi- ence, constructing a transcript captures an enormous amount that is significant—an unvoiced poignancy or irritation, a sense of loss or stark recognition marked by silence, pain and hurt conveyed in a shift to a quieter, more childlike voice.

These insights about the interviews were shared after every few interviews when we met to discuss contents and reactions in light of our guiding research objectives. This iterative process was very enriching. What was different about each interview? What clues were given by the physical surroundings and demeanour of the interviewee? What challenged our accepted views? How did particular childhood experiences impinge on current leadership styles and priorities? And so on. We were constantly pushing our own and each other's boundaries in terms of what we were hearing from our interviewees and what we made of the findings in the light of ideas and theories from other disciplines.

Most of the leaders we interviewed obviously enjoyed the process of thinking about their experiences of difference. This catalysing of their thinking was a deliberate part of our research intervention, and our method validated and encouraged them to interpret subjective experience. We wanted to put working with difference on the leadership radar screen, and we wanted to get the interviewees to connect it to their personal experience—successes as well as failures. The interview process itself helped some to talk about personal experiences of discrimination which they had hidden away but could now see were legitimate areas of managerial concern. In subsequent informal discussions with some interviewees, there seemed greater readiness to 'come out' about the ethnocentrism and racism that is prevalent in business. It felt as though we got leaders thinking about difference in a deeper and more encompassing and comprehensive way.

We each wrote sections of the initial reports (Phases 1 and 2), delivered to the productive diversity partners for discussion at workshops organised and attended by key senior staff from the Department of Immigration and Multicultural Affairs. We were both involved in giving presentations of findings at the subsequent conference and to a range of business, educational and other audiences. It has been partially due to the enthusiasm and interest generated in these forums that we decided the research findings and stories deserved a wider audience.

This book has taken the original interview data, and the culminating reports, and extended them still further into the context of leadership research and writing, primarily but not entirely in management. It is enhanced by a cross-disciplinary approach which has borrowed from psychology, sociology, post-modern theory, post-colonial theory and feminist writing, and which reflects our own backgrounds and evolving interests in the fields of leadership, identity, race and cross-cultural relations.

Bibliography

Adams, J. (1976) 'The potential for personal growth arising from inter-cultural experiences' in Adams, J., Hayes, J. and Hopson, B. *Transition: Understanding and Managing Personal Change* London: Martin Robertson.

Adler, N. (1999) 'Global leadership: women leaders' in *Advances on Global Leadership* vol. 1: 49–73, Greenwich: JAI Press.

Adler, R. (2000) 'Pigeonholed' *New Scientist* 30 September 2000: 39–41.

Adorno, T., Frenkel-Brunswik, E., Levinson, D. and R. Sanford (1950) *The Authoritarian Personality* New York: Harper.

Alex, N. (1969) *Black in Blue: A Study of Negro Policemen* New York: Appleton Century Crofts.

Allport, G. (1954) *The Nature of Prejudice* Cambridge Mass.: Addison-Wesley.

Argyris, C. (1991) 'Teaching Smart People How to Learn' *Harvard Business Review* 69(3): 99–109.

Argyris, C. and Schon, D. (1978) *Organizational Learning: A Theory of Action Perspective* Reading Mass.: Addison Wesley.

Australian Psychological Society (1997) *Racism and Prejudice: Psychological Perspectives* Melbourne: APS.

Bartlett, C. and Ghoshal, S. (2002) *Managing Across Borders: The Transnational Solution* Boston: Harvard Business School Press.

Belenky, M., Clinchy, B., Goldberger, N. and Tarule, J. (1986) *Women's Ways of Knowing: The Development of Self, Voice and Mind* New York: Basic Books.

Bell, E. (1990) 'The bicultural life experiences of career-orientated black women' *Journal of Organizational Behavior* 11: 459–77.

Bell, E. and Nkomo, S. (2001) *Our Separate Ways: Black and White Women and the Struggle for Professional Identity* Boston: Harvard Business School Press.

Bennett, J. and Bennett, M. (2001) 'Developing intercultural sensitivity: an integrative approach to global and domestic diversity', Paper presented to the Diversity Symposium, Diversity Collegium, Bentley College, Waltham, Mass., July.

Bennis, W. and Nanus, B. (1985) *Leaders: The Strategies of Taking Charge* New York: Harper and Row.

Bertone, S., Esposto, A. and R. Turner (1998) *Diversity and Dollars: Productive Diversity in Australian Business and Industry* CEDA Information Paper no. 58 Melbourne: Committee for Economic Development of Australia.

Birrell, B. and Hawthorne, L. (1997) *Immigrants and the Professions in Australia* Melbourne: Centre for Population and Urban Research, Monash University.

Blackwell, L. (1981) *Mainstreaming Outsiders: The Production of Black Professionals* New York: General Hall.

Bourdieu, P. and Passeron, J. (1977) *Reproduction in Education, Society and Culture* (trans. R. Nice) London: Sage.

Bowser, B. and Hunt, R. (eds) (1996, 2nd edn) *Impacts of Racism on White Americans* Thousand Oaks, Calif.: Sage.

Clark, C. M. H. (1981) *A History of Australia V: The People Make Laws 1888–1915* Melbourne: Melbourne University Press.

Collins, J. (2001) 'Level 5 leadership: the triumph of humility and fierce resolve' *Harvard Business Review* 79(1): 67–76.

Conger, J. (1998) 'Qualitative research as the cornerstone methodology for understanding leadership' *Leadership Quarterly* 9(1): 107–21

Cope, B. and Kalantzis, M. (2000) *A Place in the Sun: Re-creating the Australian Way of Life* Sydney: HarperCollins.

Cox, T. (1993) *Cultural Diversity in Organizations* San Francisco: Berrett Koehler.

Czarniawska-Joerges, B. (1996) 'Autobiographical acts and organizational identities' in S. Linstead, R. Grafton-Small and P. Jeffcutt (eds) *Understanding Management* London: Sage.

Dainty, P. and Andersen, M. (1996) *Managerial Capabilities* London: Macmillan.

Davidson, M. (1995) 'Living in a bi-cultural world: the role conflicts facing the black ethnic minority woman manager' *International Review of Women and Leadership* 1(1): 22–36.

Denton, T. (1990) 'Bonding and supportive relationships among black professional women: rituals of restoration' *Journal of Organizational Behavior* 11: 447–57.

Dickens, F. and Dickens, J. (1991) *The Black Manager* New York: AMACOM.

Dingle, D. (1999) *Black Enterprise Titans of the BE 100s: Black CEOs Who Redefined and Conquered American Business* New York: Wiley and Sons.

Elmes, M. and Connelley, D. (1997) 'Dreams of diversity and the realities of intergroup relations in organizations' in Prasad, P., Mills, A., Elmes, M. and A. Prasad (eds) *Managing the Organizational Melting Pot: Dilemmas of Workplace Diversity* Thousand Oaks, Calif.: Sage: 148–70.

Epstein, C. (1973) 'Positive effects on the multiple negative: explaining the success of black professional women' *American Journal of Sociology* 78(4): 912–35.

Erikson, E. H. (1968) *Identity* London: Faber & Faber.

Erickson, G. and Ernst & Young LLP (1999) *Women Entrepreneurs Only: 12 Women Entrepreneurs Tell the Stories of Their Success* New York: John Wiley.

Forster, N. (2000) 'The Myth of the International Manager' *International Journal of Human Resource Management* 11(1): 126–42.

Gardner, H. (1984, 1993) *Frames of Mind: The Theory of Multiple Intelligences* London: Fontana.

—— (1995) *Leading Minds: The Anatomy of Leadership* New York: Basic Books.

Gilligan, C. (1982) *In a Different Voice: Psychological Theory and Women's Development* Cambridge, Mass.: Harvard University Press.

Goleman, D. (1998) 'What makes a leader?' *Harvard Business Review* November–December: 93–102.

Gronn, P. (1999) *The Making of Educational Leaders* London: Cassell.

Hage, G. (1998) *White Nation: Fantasies of White Supremacy in a Multicultural Society* Sydney: Pluto Press.

Hambrick, D., Davison, S., Snell, S. and C. Snow (1994) *When Groups Consist of Multiple Nationalities: Towards a New Understanding of the Implications* Lexington, Mass.: International Consortium for Executive Development.

Hawthorne, L. (1988) *Making It in Australia* Melbourne: Edward Arnold.

—— (1994) *Labour Market Barriers for Immigrant Engineers in Australia* Canberra: AGPS.

—— (1996) 'Reversing past stereotypes: skilled NESB women in Australia' *Journal of Intercultural Studies* 17(1): 41–52.

Hearn, J. and Parkin, W. (2001) *Gender, Sexuality and Violence in Organizations* London: Sage.

Heifetz, R. and Laurie, D. (1997) 'The work of leadership' *Harvard Business Review* 75(1): 124–34.

—— (1999) 'Mobilizing adaptive work: beyond visionary leadership' in Conger, J. et. al. *The Change Leader's Handbook* San Francisco: Jossey Bass.

Helms, J. (ed.) (1990) *Black and White Racial Identity: Theory, Research and Practice* Westport, Conn.: Greenwood Press.

Hofstede, G. (1980) *Culture's Consequences: International Differences in Work Related Values* Beverly Hills, Calif.: Sage.

—— (1981) *Cultures and Organizations: Softwares of the Mind* Berkshire, UK: McGraw Hill.

Hudson, L. (1966) *Contrary Imaginations: A Psychological Study of the English Schoolboy* Harmondsworth: Penguin.

Jackall, R. (1988) *Moral Mazes: The World of Corporate Managers* New York: Oxford University Press.

Jayasuriya, L., and Kee, P. (1999) *The Asianisation of Australia: Some Facts About the Myths* Melbourne: Melbourne University Press.

Jung, D., and Avolio, B. (1999) 'Effects of leadership style and followers' cultural orientation on performance in group and individual task conditions' *Academy of Management Journal* 42(2): 208–18.

Jupp, J. (1989) 'The ethnic composition of Australian elites' in Jupp, J.(ed.) *The Challenge of Diversity* Canberra: Office of Multicultural Affairs, AGPS.

Kalantzis, M., Cope, B., Lo Bianco, J., Morgan, B. and A. Lohrey (1993) 'Australia 2001: unity through diversity' Occasional Paper 14, NLLIA Centre for Workplace Communication and Culture, Sydney.

Kanter, R. (1997) *Rosabeth Moss Kanter on the Frontiers of Management* Boston: Harvard Business School Press.

Kets de Vries, M. and Florent-Treacy, E. (1999) *The New Global Leaders* San Francisco, Jossey Bass.

Kirkpatrick, S. and Locke, E. (1991) 'Leadership: Do traits matter?' *Academy of Management Executive* 5(2).

Klein, N. (2000) *No Logo* London: Flamingo.

Knights, D. and Morgan, G. 'Leadership and corporate strategy: toward a critical analysis' *Leadership Quarterly* 3(3): 171–90.

Kotter, J. (1988) *The Leadership Factor* New York: The Free Press.

—— (1990) *A Force for Change: How Leadership Differs from Management* New York: The Free Press.

Kouzes, J. and Posner, M. (1987) *The Leadership Challenge: How to Get Extraordinary Things Done in Organizations* San Francisco: Jossey Bass.

Levitt, T. (1983) 'The globalization of markets' *Harvard Business Review* May–June.

Light, I. And Gold, S. (2000) *Ethnic Economies* San Diego: Academic Press.

Linnehan, F. and Konrad, A. (1999) 'Diluting diversity: implications for intergroup inequality in organizations' *Journal of Management Inquiry* 8(4): 399–414.

Little, G. (1992) 'The uses of childhood' Paper delivered at the International Society of Political Psychology, San Francisco.

—— (1999) 'Middle way leaders' Paper delivered at the International Society of Political Psychology, Amsterdam.

—— (1999) *The Public Emotions* Sydney: ABC Books.

Maccoby, M. (1976) *The Gamesman: The New Corporate Leaders* New York: Simon and Schuster.

—— (2000) 'Narcissistic leaders: The incredible pros and the inevitable cons' *Harvard Business Review* January–February: 69–77.

Macintyre, S. (1985) *Winners and Losers: The Pursuit of Social Justice in Australian History* Sydney: Allen and Unwin.

Mant, A. (1983) *Leaders We Deserve* Oxford: Basil Blackwell.

—— (1997) *Intelligent Leadership* Sydney: Allen & Unwin.

Meindl, J., Erlich, S. and Dukerich, J. (1985) 'The romance of leadership' in *Administrative Science Quarterly* 30: 78–102.

Mighty, E. J. (1997) 'Triple jeopardy: immigrant women of color in the labor force' in Prasad, P., Mills, A., Elmes, M. and A. Prasad (eds) *Managing the Organizational Melting Pot: Dilemmas of Workplace Diversity* Thousand Oaks, Calif.: Sage: 312–39.

Miller, J. B. (1986) *Toward a New Psychology of Women* London: Penguin.

Mitscherlich, A. (1963, trans 1969) *Society Without the Father: A Contribution to Social Psychology* London: Tavistock.

Morrison, A. (1992) *The New Leaders: Guidelines on Leadership Diversity in America* San Francisco: Jossey Bass.

—— (1995) 'Taking charge of developing diversity' training materials for *Taking Charge of Developing Diversity* March, California.

Morrison, A., White, R. and Van Velsor (1987) *Breaking the Glass Ceiling* Reading, Mass., Addison Wesley.

Oliver, R. (2000) 'New rules for global markets' *Journal of Business Strategy* May/June.

Parry, K. (1998) 'Grounded theory and social process: a new direction for leadership research' *Leadership Quarterly* 9(1): 85–105.

Prasad, A. (1997) 'The colonising consciousness and representations of the other: a postcolonial critique of the discourse of oil' in Prasad, P., Mills, A., Elmes, M. and A. Prasad (eds) *Managing the Organizational Melting Pot: Dilemmas of Workplace Diversity* Thousand Oaks, Calif.: Sage: 285–311.

Prasad, P., Mills, A., Elmes, M. and Prasad, A. (eds) *Managing the Organizational Melting Pot: Dilemmas of Workplace Diversity*, Thousand Oaks, Calif.: Sage.

Pringle, J. and Collins, S. (1996) 'Pakeha women-run organisations: glimpses of form and style' in Olsson, S. and Stirton, N. (eds) *International Women and Leadership Conference Proceedings* Massey University, Palmerston North: 407–25.

Pringle, J. and Scowcroft, J. (1996) 'Managing diversity: meaning and practice in New Zealand organisations *Asia Pacific Journal of Human Resources* 34(2): 28–43.

Quy Nguyen Huy (1999) 'Emotional capability, emotional intelligence and radical change' *Academy of Management Review* 24(2): 325–45.

Reynolds, H. (1999) *Why Weren't We Told* Melbourne: Penguin.

Reynolds, K. and Turner, J. (2000) 'Prejudice as a group process: the role of social identity' in Augoustinos, M. and Reynolds, K. (eds) *Us and Them: Understanding the Psychology of Prejudice and Racism* London: Sage.

Riesman, D. with Glazer, N. and Denney, R. (1961) *The Lonely Crowd: A Study of the Changing American Character* New Haven, Conn.: Yale University Press.

Riley, M. (2001) 'Flat Jac' *The Age* 11 August: 1 (Business and Money).

Rosen, R. (2000) *Global Literacies: Lessons on Business Leadership and National Cultures* New York: Simon and Schuster.

Rothman, R. (1993, 2nd edn) *Inequality and Stratification: Class, Color and Gender* New Jersey: Prentice Hall.

Russakoff, D. (2001) 'Pride and Prejudice' *The Age* 30 September: 1 (reproduced from *Washington Post Magazine*).

Senge, P. (1990) *The Fifth Discipline: The Art and Practice of the Learning Organization* New York: Random House.

Sennett, R. (1998) *The Corrosion of Character: The Personal Consequences of Work in the New Capitalism* New York: Norton.

Shamir, B. (1995) 'Social distance and charisma: theoretical notes and an exploratory study' *Leadership Quarterly* 6(1): 19–47.

Simpson, G (1984) 'The daughters of Charlotte Ray: the career development process during the exploratory and establishment stages of black women attorneys' *Sex Roles* 11: 113–39.

Sinclair, A. (1991) 'After excellence: models of organisational culture for the public sector' *Australian Journal of Public Administration* 50(3): 321–32.

—— (1992) 'The tyranny of a team ideology' *Organization Studies* 13(4): 611–26.

—— (1994) *Trials at the Top: Chief Executives Talk about Men, Women and the Australian Executive Culture* Melbourne: The Australian Centre.

——. (1995) 'The seduction of the self-managed team' *Leading and Managing* 1(1): 44–62.

—— (1998) *Doing Leadership Differently: Gender, Power and Sexuality in a Changing Business Culture* Melbourne: Melbourne University Press.

——. (2000) 'Women within diversity: risks and possibilities' *Women in Management Review* Special Issue 15 (5/6).

Sinclair, A. and Britton Wilson, V. (1999) *The Culture Inclusive Classroom: Perspectives from Management Education* Melbourne: Melbourne Business School.

Steinberg, Blema (1998) 'The making of women presidents and prime ministers: the impact of birth order, sex of siblings and parent–daughter dynamics', paper presented to the Annual Meeting of the International Society of Political Psychology, 11–15 June, Montreal.

Thomas, D. and Gabarro, J. (1999) *Breaking Through: The Making of Minority Executives in Corporate America* Boston: Harvard Business School Press.

Thompson, E. (1994) *Fair Enough: Egalitarianism in Australia* Sydney: University of New South Wales Press.

Trompenaars, F. and Hampden-Turner, C. (2002) *21 Leaders for the 21st Century: How Innovative Leaders Manage in the Digital Age* New York: McGraw Hill.

Tsui, A. and Gutek, B. (1999) *Demographic Differences in Organizations: Current Research and Future Directions* Lanham, US: Lexington Books.

Volet, S. (1999) 'Motivation within and across cultural-educational contexts' *Advances in Motivation and Achievement*: 11 Greenwich, Conn.: JAI Press: 185–231.

Watson, I. (1996) *Opening the Glass Door: Overseas-born Managers in Australia* Canberra: AGPS.

Weick, K. (1995) *Sense-making in Organizations* Thousand Oaks Calif.: Sage.

Whyte, W. (1959) *Man and Organization: Three Problems in Human Relations in Industry* Irwin.

Winnicott, D. (1971/91) *Playing and Reality* London: Routledge.

Wong-Ming Ji, D. and Mir, A. (1997) 'How international is international management? Provincialism, parochialism and the problematic of global diversity' in Prasad, P., Mills, A., Elmes, M. and A. Prasad (eds) *Managing the Organizational Melting Pot: Dilemmas of Workplace Diversity* Thousand Oaks, Calif.: Sage: 340–66.

Young, I. (1990) *Justice and the Politics of Difference* Princeton: Princeton University Press.

Yukl, G. (1994) *Leadership in Organizations* New York: Prentice Hall.

Zaleznik, A. (1977) 'Managers and Leaders: Are they different?' *Harvard Business Review* 55(2): 67–78.

Index

race, 93, 115, 117; interracial fluency, 115; *see also* identity
racism, 31-2, 49, 70, 90-1, 105-8, 115
recruitment, 92
reflectiveness, 59
relationships, 22, 23
research method and sample, 12, 19, 122
Reynolds, H., 108
Reynolds, K., 103
Rice, C., 115
Riesman, D., 23
Riley, M., 114
risk, appetite for, 60, 63-5
roots, 12, 13, 15-40, 114; *see also* backgrounds; childhood; families
Rosen, R., 2, 12, 115
Rothman, R., 115
routes, 2, 5, 41-56, 114; *see also* head path; heart path; pathways
Russakoff, D., 115

schooling, 26
self-censorship *see* censorship
Sennett, R., 102, 103
sexism, 91, 107
Shamir, B., 11
siblings, 6, 24, 33-4
Simon, D., 72
Sinclair, A., 28, 44, 88, 99, 100, 104, 113, 115
social skills, 37
socialisation *see* backgrounds
sport, 37, 46, 48-9, 91
Steinberg, B., 24

stereotypes, stereotyping, 31, 50-1, 82, 107, 116, 117
supports, supportive factors, 46-7

teams: diverse/multicultural, 83; homogenous, 79, 85; orientation/culture of, 50, 65
tolerance, 105, 108
Thomas, D. and Gabarro, J., 18, 89
Thompson, E., 106, 107
tokenism, 80, 91
transcultural competence, 116-17
Trompenaars, F. and Hampden-Turner, C., 12, 116
trust, 41, 52-3, 54

values, 16, 43, 120
visibility, heightened, 82, 88, 91
vision, 2

Watson, I., 92, 103
Weick, K., 28
White Australia policy, 32, 106
Whyte, W., 111
Winnicott, D., 53
wives, influence of, 38, 43
women, 22, 26, 42, 71, 83, 91
Wong-Ming Ji, D., 110
World Economic Forum, 99

Young, I., 109
Yukl, G., 11

Zaleznik, A., 55